THE DESIGN OF DEVELOPMENT

THE Design OF

Development

BY JAN TINBERGEN

THE ECONOMIC

DEVELOPMENT

INSTITUTE

International Bank for
Reconstruction and Development

THE JOHNS HOPKINS PRESS, Baltimore, *1958*

Foreword

BY THE DIRECTOR OF THE
ECONOMIC DEVELOPMENT INSTITUTE

This is the second publication of the Economic Development Institute. The Institute was established in 1955 by the International Bank for Reconstruction and Development. Its essential objective is to improve the quality of economic management in government in the less developed countries. At the Institute, senior officials of member governments of the Bank are given an opportunity to study and discuss the practical problems facing them as administrators as well as the larger features of the economic landscape which their immersion in the rushing stream of day-to-day tasks often prevents their seeing clearly. An effort is made to put before them the growing experience of the Bank and of the international community as a whole in promoting economic development.

Publications of the Economic Development Institute are primarily designed for use by persons working in responsible administrative and advisory capacities in government, financial institutions or other important sectors of the economy of the Bank's less developed countries. It is hoped that they may also prove informative and useful to educational institutions and groups and organizations of all kinds concerned with the problems of economic development.

The publications are the work of individuals. While in every case inestimable benefit has been derived from intimate contact with the work of the Bank, the publications in no sense purport to set forth the official views of the Bank or to be an authoritative statement of its policies in general or in detail.

This study by Professor Jan Tinbergen, of the Netherlands School of Economics, Rotterdam, was prepared in 1955 at the request of Mr. Leonard Rist, Economic Director of the World Bank. It has been used extensively at the Institute as a basis for discussions of development policies and problems of programming and project appraisal. It is being published in the belief that it will be of interest and value to a wider audience.

Michael L. Hoffman

Contents

THE DESIGN OF DEVELOPMENT

CHAPTER I The Elements of

Development Policy

I I *Introductory*

Economic development is increasingly felt to be a necessity for a number of countries which are suffering from a low level of material well-being. In the presently advanced countries, the process of economic development was carried on by large numbers of individual entrepreneurs. Government action, although sometimes important, was restricted in scope, often limited to providing transportation facilities. Decisions were taken on the basis of vague ideas of general progress, and often somewhat haphazardly. The process was not an even one, but was interrupted by setbacks and crises; and probably quite a good deal of misplaced energy and effort went into over-investments. In many respects development was a process of trial and error.

It is now believed that economic development may be furthered by what may be called a "development policy." This certainly does not mean that no use would be made of the powerful force of private initiative; but it is hoped that some of the errors and waste of the past may be avoided. This development policy would have four principal objectives:

(i)   To create the general conditions favorable to development;
(ii) To acquaint the government itself, the business community and the public generally with the potentialities and advantages of development;

(iii)   To make a number of investments, usually of the "basic" type; and

(iv)   To take measures designed to facilitate and to stimulate private activity and investment.

We may say that (ii) will result in the projection of a *pattern* of development, whereas (iii) may be said to represent the government investment *program,* or *plan,* consisting of a number of *public projects.* In order that the pattern may materialize, a number of *private projects* will also have to be carried out. Activity (iv), the *policy* in the narrower sense of the word, is an attempt to induce action by the private sector in conformity with the pattern. In this paper, "program" is used to refer to the total of desired investment, both public and private, unless the context indicates that only public investment is meant, and "programming" accordingly refers to programming for the whole of the economy.

In this introductory chapter a few remarks will be made on the nature of each of the objectives of development policy and their interdependence.

I 2   *The Creation of the General Conditions
        for Development*

In order that sustained development may take place, an economy must possess certain basic characteristics. Among these are a minimum of security and stability, both in general and particularly with respect to economic matters. There must be some government activity of the sort usually considered essential to an orderly state, such as the maintenance of order and of physical security of persons and property. In addition, there must be a minimum of "instruments of economic policy" in the hands of the government, and these must be properly used. For example, the financial and monetary policy must be such that serious inflation as well as deflation is avoided. Inflation may upset the economy by introducing an element of uncertainty and unreliability into economic calculations, and by causing misdirection of productive resources. In particular, inflation creates an opportunity for speculation and the acquisition of high incomes by persons who do not make productive contributions to the economy; this results in a greater demand for luxuries than can be satisfied by an optimum use of the factors of production. Also there will be a tendency towards balance of payments disequilibrium, resulting in currency regulations, which are often discriminatory and not in the general interest.

Another general task of the government is to provide a minimum of social security and to correct the most extreme inequalities in income—inequalities easily conducive to social unrest and lack of cooperative spirit in production.

Finally, a very important condition for development is the provision of training and education at all levels. Since these activities are not as a rule considered a part of economic policy, they will not be considered in this report, but their importance should not be overlooked.

I 3   *Awareness of Development Potentialities*
        and Advantages

Awareness of the possibilities of development is accomplished largely through statistics, research and information. First come the basic activities consisting of the collection of statistics and the making of surveys. On their data must be based the diversified activities called programming; these are discussed in some detail later in this report. The results of statistical investigation and programming must be communicated to those concerned with development together with facts about government policies; here the provision of adequate information is of importance.

The basic statistical orientation must consist, first of all, of reliable statistics on such subjects as production, trade, prices, government finance, income and income distribution. In addition to this a summary of the structure of the economy must be prepared, taking the well established form of national income estimates and national accounts. Even if the basic material is incomplete or unreliable in certain respects an attempt should be made to arrive at such a summary.

Programming may take a form ranging from one sheet of tentative figures on a country's future income and investment to a series of reports on all industries and contemplated projects involved for the next decade. Programs by their very nature have to be guesses and must be revised periodically. Perhaps their most important contribution is that they try to show the interdependence of the relevant economic phenomena. Even those programs are useful which do no more than show in the most elementary way that the rise in income must bear some relation to the volume of investment, and that incomes must not be expended in a manner and for purposes which may cause inflation. Of course, the more detailed they are, the more guidance they will provide to the business community, where they may serve as the basis for market research.

I 4   *Basic Government Investments*

For a country to be stable and to offer a basis for economic activity and development, a certain number of fundamental investments must be made. There must be a minimum of housing and transportation facilities. Supplies of power and water must be available, land may have to be reclaimed or irrigated and so on. Usually such investments cannot all be made by private individuals, since their yields spread through the community and do not readily take the form of income to the investor. The extent of these facilities should of course have some relation to the volume of production of the consuming industries, and the investments should therefore be planned on the basis of the general development to be expected. There may be some difference of opinion about the exact dividing line between public and private activity in these fields; this question is discussed later on.

I 5   *Measures to Facilitate and Stimulate Private Activity*

In certain circumstances, the emphasis will have to be shifted towards a more indirect type of policy, designed to facilitate and stimulate private activity. This does not mean that public investment will not have to continue. But the policy as a whole will have to become more subtle and use more instruments. It will have to be based on more elaborate programming. Instruments of tax policy, both direct and indirect, import duties or subventions will have to be employed, and representatives of certain industries will have to be approached directly. The use of these devices will have to be judged against the background of the general policies referred to in Section I 2, so that a co-ordinated series of objectives can be achieved by the simultaneous application of a variety of instruments of economic policy.

In the next few chapters the various elements of development policy proper will be taken up in succession.

I 6   *Development Policy Under Varying Circumstances*

Depending on circumstances some elements of development policy will require more emphasis and attention or will appear more or less promising than others.

If a country finds itself in a state of *severe inflation,* attention may have to be directed to the proper general policy before embarking on new and ambitious programs or policies.

In an early stage of development, more emphasis may have to be laid on basic investments, perhaps those designed to eliminate economic bottle necks. In later more mature stages, the stimulation of private investment may come more into the foreground. To what extent this will be at all possible and promising will also depend on the general attitude of the population with regard to development and to government measures, and on the quality of the administrative apparatus. The details of development policy will be governed by the structure of the country's economy, as determined by its natural resources, climate and geographical situation, as well as by temporary bottlenecks that may arise.

Finally, the size of the country should be mentioned as a factor. In a small country, it may require so few persons to design and execute a policy that it becomes relatively easy to accomplish the orientation, co-ordination, persuasion and co-operation so important for successful development. This applies in particular, as will be clear, to the role that may be played by general advisors from foreign countries.

CHAPTER II The Essence of Programming

II 1   *Nature of General Programming*

From the discussion in Chapter I it will have become clear that a policy of deliberate development, to be successful, must satisfy a number of important conditions. Any action on a large scale requires careful preparation, and this is unquestionably true in the formulation of development policy. Preparation is of course a prerequisite to the numerous practical decisions to be taken by the technicians and organizers of the separate projects, but it is likewise needed at an earlier stage. To assure consistency and to avoid large-scale waste and disorganization, care should be taken that the component parts of the program form a coherent and co-ordinated whole. It is the purpose of general programming to see to this coherence and co-ordination. General programming has to supply a bird's-eye view of the pattern of future development of the country, and to show the possible and the most desirable development of the national product and its components, i.e., imports and production of the broad industrial groups, as well as its destination: exports, consumption, investment and government use.

Certain techniques, mainly of a statistical nature, including the use of mathematics, have been developed during the last few decades to arrive at the necessary estimates. These techniques will be briefly discussed in this chapter. But it must first be made clear that programming is not an alternative to common sense; it cannot replace common sense and it should not. It does supplement it, particularly with regard to the orders of magnitude of the phenomena involved. In the design of development all information and all methods available should be put to use. This seems the more desirable since information of the traditional type, the usual statistics, is often insufficient and inconsistent. Anything helping to supplement it should be welcomed. The general methods now under discussion sometimes make it possible also to derive new insight from figures about other more or less comparable countries. Certain patterns of reaction, both in the field of consumption and in that of production, appear to show regularities which may be of help in forecasting possible development.

One of the most typical elements which programming is able to add to factual information may be called "consistency." The figures for the development of the individual industries have to obey a number of conditions of consistency. The total resources—land, capital, skilled labor—to be employed by them together cannot exceed the available quantities of these resources. Quantities produced have to be sold; in order that they may be sold their prices have to satisfy certain conditions; and these prices are dependent on the prices of land, capital and labor. Imports are needed; but they must be paid for by exports or by the importation of capital, and so on. The activities of certain industries have to be interrelated, since one uses the products of the other, or since both supply products to a third. Taxes collected by the government, together with loans and deficit financing, will have to cover the total expenditure planned. Programming tries to establish a set of figures satisfying all these conditions. If the provisional program taken as a point of departure cannot possibly be brought into line with such requirements, it will have to be revised. Large practical errors may be avoided if such revisions are made in advance and are not forced upon the policymaker by unexpected events. This is what programming tries to avoid.

Apart from the element of consistency, programming also tries
to give some guidance as to the *completeness* of the picture. It helps
to reveal which elements of information are lacking and gives hints
as to where to look for these elements. More specifically, it leads to
inquiries as to where the particular skills needed and where the
willingness to take initiative are to be found.

II 2   *Rough Outline of General Programming*

The aim of general programming is to arrive at a framework of
figures for the possible development of an economy.

The possibilities for development are dependent on certain factors such as the willingness of the government and the people to
make special efforts, on foreign assistance in the field of investment
or education, and on a number of short-term factors, such as crop
yields, world market fluctuations, etc. In order to show what influence can be exerted by changes in such factors it is often useful to
draw up a number of *alternative programs,* each of them based on
specified assumptions. The existence of an alternative program will
be very useful if some of the factors turn out to be less favorable, or
more favorable than was originally anticipated. This procedure of
using alternatives may, in addition, be applied in order to illustrate
the influence of uncertainties in some of the data. Each of the
alternative programs will have to be calculated with the aid of the
same techniques, now to be described. These techniques are based
on certain relationships between economic and other phenomena
which have been tested, to a greater or lesser extent, by statistical
research, and on a number of basic economic "laws," with which an
equilibrated economic development must comply. Usually a first
outline is derived from "macro-economic" figures; this is then refined in a second, "micro-economic" program. A macro-economic
program merely projects the development of such general totals as
national income and outlay (private consumption and investment

and public outlay), imports, exports and imports of capital, and total national capital. A micro-economic program fills in this framework with figures in individual industries, and, as the case may require, on regions or even specific important plants.

The *macro-economic* program is usually based on a forecast of population over the period to be studied, say ten years. Both total population and active population are estimated. An assumption is then made as to the growth of productivity, i.e., product per active person. This assumption may play one of two roles. On the one hand it may be—since productivity is decisive for income per head—an indication of the development in material well-being it is desired to attain; on the other hand, it may be an indicator of what is assumed to be possible. Here the alternatives already discussed may have to be distinguished. Statistical experience has shown that over longer periods of time this growth has been rather stable, the most common figure, taking the average for all industries of a country, being 1.5 per cent per annum. There may be special reasons, e.g., in the case of the recovery of a war-damaged economy, to assume higher figures. Higher figures may also be used where the government proposes to make a special effort. In such a case it should be made clear, however, what the usual figure has been and to what extent a special effort is being demanded. Multiplying the "active population" figure by "productivity" will give the volume of gross product or "total resources available." It is these resources that will be available under the hypotheses made—indicating either the most probable rate of development or the most desirable one, or the rate to be expected if specified events occur.

A rough estimate of the volume of *imports* may then be made, based on the average import content of the country's product—an estimate which will have to be revised as soon as some insight has been gained as to the composition of future national product. With certain further assumptions as to possible capital imports, an estimate of the necessary exports follows. The question whether these exports can be sold and at what prices is an important element of programming. The value of national resources minus imports equals national income and with the aid of tax rates and a savings rate it may very roughly be estimated how tax revenue and savings are likely to develop.

One vital problem may now be considered: will savings plus estimated capital imports be sufficient to raise the national capital to the extent required to attain the assumed national income?

The relationships which are relevant to this question have been dealt with in a concise and simple way by the introduction of the so-called *"capital coefficient."* Experience shows that, at least for countries, the ratio between investments and the resulting increase in net national income varies less than was long believed. Something can be said about its order of magnitude, although the margin of uncertainty is still fairly high. Or, to put it in a different way: there appears to be a fairly constant ratio between a country's wealth and its income per annum. For economies like the United States and the United Kingdom, ratios of about three to one have been found to obtain over a remarkably long period. It is often maintained that for new investments in underdeveloped countries a higher ratio should be expected, since there must be established a number of basic facilities which are relatively "capital-intensive" in most countries. On the other hand, there are examples (e.g., Mexico) of recent developments showing an even lower capital coefficient. It would seem often safe to assume that for development programs a capital coefficient of 4 is needed, but we will also consider the consequences of lower values, even down to 2. The historical record of any given country will be the best guide, provided that it covers a sufficiently long period.

The significance and limitations of the application of capital coefficients will be discussed somewhat more thoroughly in Annex v i. For the moment the existence of a roughly constant ratio of this kind will be taken for granted. Its meaning is that the annual percentage increase in national income to be obtained from a program of investment of, say, 8 per cent of national income amounts to 2 to 4 per cent. From a program of 12 per cent—an ambitious one for many countries—a 3 to 6 per cent annual increase in national income will be obtained. Now, the aim of development is not simply to increase national income but also to increase national income per capita and at a fairly fast rate. If there is an annual increase of 1 per cent in population, however, an increase of 1 per cent in national income does not increase income per capita. Several countries show population increases of 2 to 3 per cent annually. It follows that a rate of investment of 2 to 12 per cent is needed merely to maintain the level of income per head: 2 per cent in the favorable case of a 1 per cent population increase with a capital coefficient of 2; 12 per cent, however, in the unfavorable case of a population increase of 3 per cent with a capital coefficient of 4. With the assumed population growth of 1 per cent per annum, and an objective of an increase of income per capita at the rate of 3 per cent, which is modest if a real change is wanted, an investment program of 8 to 16 per cent would be needed. Even with a rate of growth of 3 per cent per annum it would take two decades before the average income of South Asia is brought to the modest level of Mexico's.

More generally, to raise income per head by 3 per cent a year requires an investment program of at least 2 and perhaps 4 times $(x + 3)$ per cent of national income, where x is the rate of increase in population.

A study of actual figures for most countries discloses that the above analysis sets a lower limit to development programs which may well be, at the same time, about the maximum attainable in the short-run. For the numerous countries with a 2.5 per cent rate of population growth programs of 11 to 22 per cent would follow; for the principal countries in South Asia with population increases of 1 to 1.5 per cent, programs of 8 to 18 per cent of national income would follow, well above what has so far been possible. This underlines the urgency of the tasks ahead, not only for the governments concerned, but also for the international community as a whole. At the same time the figures presented illustrate, more eloquently than words, the importance of checks on the increase in population. Any reduction in percentage population increase means a two- to four-fold reduction in the rate of savings needed to achieve a given rise in the standard of living.

From the examples cited, another feature of the process of development becomes apparent, namely, that small changes in the savings ratio, if it is modest, may either bring the country from a state of stagnation into one of development or the other way round. If a country's population is growing at the rate of 1.5 per cent a year, and if again the capital coefficient is taken to be 4, then a savings rate of 6 per cent means stagnation, whereas a rate of 8 per cent means an increase in income per capita of 0.5 per cent annually.

It may be necessary, even at this stage, to take account of the *time-lags* involved in the execution of larger investment projects. The relation between total product and total capital refers to capital in the form of productive equipment and stocks ready for use. Production of investment goods will have to start early enough to allow for the length of the production process. Accordingly, investment activity in a given year may be partly dictated by the capital needs in some future year. This is of particular importance when a long period of construction is involved as, e.g., in the case of large dams or mine pits. In the stage of macro-planning, it may be sufficient to adopt an average time-lag for all investment activity. Later on, in the stage of micro-planning, a more precise calculation, depending on the type of investment activity, will be needed.

The long time needed for the execution of certain investment projects is also reflected in the existence of a large volume of works in progress and commitments to finish them which considerably narrow down, in each year, the possibility of starting new projects. Only a relatively modest part of the necessary equipment and labor is released for such new projects.

A word may be added about the *statistical sources* to be used in deriving the coefficients needed in programming. Preferably as much information as possible should be taken from the historical record of the country itself, provided that a sufficiently long period is covered. Coefficients on import content or capital coefficients should not be derived on the basis of a few years only, since there are considerable random fluctuations in annual figures. Averages over some ten years are often safer, since they also rule out possible cyclical influences. If no such figures are available, figures for comparable countries may be used; even comparability is not essential if general research has shown that there are no marked differences between countries. Certain statistical regularities are quite general indeed, such as, e.g., the distribution of expenditures over various categories or the capital coefficient. General though they may be, the coefficients are not too precisely known and their margin of uncertainty often is more important than their systematic variation from one country to another. This again stresses the desirability of working with alternative programs.

II   3   *Projection of a Country's Markets*

The next stage of programming, the "micro" stage, will then be reached, in trying to answer the question: what types of goods will have to be produced? This different question must, in principle, be considered from two angles, well known to the economist: "demand" and "supply." To begin with, we assume—for the time being that prices will not change. What then are the sales of the various classes of goods to be expected? There are two markets to be considered, home and abroad. Home demand derives from the increasing national income. We know something about how an increased income is spent: relatively fewer "necessities," more "luxuries." This tendency is international and indications can be derived, in this case, from foreign statistics. Numerous studies with respect to foreign demand are available, showing how increased foreign incomes are being spent. Of course, the "art" of such an analysis is to find figures that cover the most comparable groups of people in other countries. And common sense, as has already been stressed, is always needed to correct any estimate.

Generally speaking, there are three sources of data on demand for final consumer goods. The first source is *family budget* statistics. These data are obtained from a relatively small number of families, which may mean a large margin of error; in addition, there will be a bias, to the extent that families willing to provide this information may have a spending pattern different from other families. Usually family budget statistics give a detailed list of the goods bought, and in this respect they are, in principle, complete. In addition, they give quantities bought or amounts spent for different income classes, showing the influence of income on demand. It must also be kept in mind that total demand for a certain commodity is exerted not only by "families in existence" but also by "families in preparation," i.e., engaged couples buying furniture, etc. Finally, there may be industrial demand and institutional demand (schools, hotels, shipping companies, etc.).

The second source for final demand data may be direct observation of *retail trade.* From this source, total demand for a country may be derived, without data on its distribution over different income groups.

The same is true for the third source of demand data, that calculated from *production, imports* and *exports* and, where appropriate, changes in *stocks.* In this case, the influence exerted by changes in income can be ascertained only by comparisons for different years (if national income is known year by year) or as between countries (if national income is known country by country).[1] The advantage of the figures of the second and third sources is their completeness: neither, and particularly not the third source, is based on samples, but each covers the whole of consumption.

---

[1] A continuous flow of new investigations is gradually narrowing down the uncertainties in our knowledge on the spending of income and also attempting to discover the similarities and dissimilarities between countries. An example is Colin Clark, *Conditions of Economic Progress,* 2nd Edition, London 1951.

The relation between income and expenditure over a period does not necessarily correspond to that revealed by family budget statistics. It may vary with time. Demand changes from year to year may be called short-term changes. If incomes fall there will, e.g., be a tendency to maintain demand for necessities and to reduce demand for luxuries and durables, which might be called postponable demand. Long-term adaptations of demand to a changed income will, however, also have to reserve some income for durables. It may be assumed that comparisons between demand of different income classes as found in family budget statistics, will reveal something about such long-term adaptations.

Market projections have some particular importance for arriving at a reasonable estimate of what is possible in the field of *import substitution*. In a growing economy, an increasing number of products, formerly imported, may be produced at home as soon as a sufficient volume of sales are reached by a plant of optimum size. This process of import substitution should, however, not diverge too much from what a reasonable international division of labor suggests, a point to be discussed subsequently. Substitution may take place gradually, as resources become available. For example, if wire is being imported, efforts may first be made to produce wire locally from imported rods; only at a later stage, when sufficient new capital is available, will it be possible for the rods themselves to be produced at home.

The most difficult part of the analysis comes with consideration of international competition. Thus far it has been assumed that prices do not change. This implies that the quantities demanded can be supplied at unchanged prices. Probably this is not true. Every country has particular industries in which production is relatively cheap, others in which it is expensive. This brings us to the cost side of the problem. At what prices can increased quantities be supplied? In principle, the individual industrial projects known to the administration have to supply the answer. To the extent that such projects are known, some provisional answer will be possible.

If the price at which a product can be supplied in future is higher than the existing level, demand will be less; if the price is lower, demand will be greater than was initially estimated. We have to know demand elasticities in order to tell by how much the initial estimates will have to be corrected. Sometimes we know these elasticities. Here again, international comparisons will be a useful source of knowledge.

Our knowledge both of possible future production costs and demand elasticity is very incomplete, however. The set of individual industrial projects available will, as a rule, not cover all industries and products. Some sectors may be fairly completely covered by the projects available, others only partly so or not at all. It may be wise to consider each type of sector separately. We shall have to supplement the limited knowledge derived from the projects by reasonable guesses, which will no doubt turn out to be to some extent erroneous. This state of affairs is not new at all, but merely confronts the programmer with the fact of "incomplete information" so familiar to employers. The production pattern must then be estimated; it should include all practicable possibilities for producing relatively cheaply and, in fields for which no cost figures are available, should assume expanded production in proportion to demand increases, as far as production factors are available.

The principle upon which the selection of the goods to be supplied rests is the well-known principle of comparative cost. Each country should produce the goods in which it has the greatest comparative advantages in costs. This will maximize national as well as international production, under certain conditions, to be sure. These conditions are discussed in Section IV 4, where commercial policy is considered. For the most appropriate choice of goods we may then rely on this aim of maximum contribution to national product. The resulting "tests" are discussed in Chapter III.

The elements so far presented lead to a fairly complicated mechanism of interdependencies, but do not give a complete picture of the complications. Two other important phenomena should be mentioned. As already observed, export commodities must satisfy two conditions: they should be sufficient to meet import needs, (apart from imports of capital, etc.) and they should actually be saleable. Each new addition to production facilities itself requires production of the investment goods involved. If additional shoe production is needed, it must be preceded by construction of the shoe factory. This itself requires activity by the building trade and by say, toolmakers, and these activities must be inserted in the program. In addition, some time will elapse between the start of construction and completion of the factory. Such "time-lags" must also be taken into account, as emphasized in Section II 2.

The methods that may be employed to make up a program satisfying all the conditions of an economic and a technical character summarized thus far range from primitive trial-and-error to highly sophisticated mathematical techniques. Choice of methods depends upon experts and the nature of the data available. The annual programming of the British economy has been done with the aid of trial-and-error methods rather than mathematical procedures, whereas the latter have been more to the foreground in the Netherlands. Recently, Professor Frisch made use of some of the most modern techniques in advising on Indian development programs. Among the scientific tools he uses is the so-called "linear programming," a technique increasingly applied in private business. It is designed to establish production programs consistent with the requirements of inter-industry supplies. If a need develops for applying this technique, experts should be called in.

II 4   *The Role to be Played by Individual Projects*

As is self-evident, any pattern of future production must ultimately materialize as a set of individual projects, largely in the private sphere. Here we arrive at the very essence of the development phenomenon. One of the reasons why development has not been achieved in a number of countries is the absence of sufficient spontaneous projects of the requisite kind. Development policy should aim at inducing private producers and investors to undertake them. The methods that may be used to bring this about are discussed in Chapter IV.

The role to be played by individual projects in making up the general pattern of development is to provide information, even if only scattered, on the costs of production of specified commodities. Two main difficulties are encountered by the programming agency. First, for the projects to be helpful at all, they must be sound. Their soundness will have to be tested. Secondly, they are too few and the question therefore arises whether they can be "constructed" with the help of general information of the type available to the programming agencies. The two questions are related. Part of the testing will consist of finding out whether a program "fits" in the general picture of the country's development. This requires consideration of the development of markets and the testing of cost estimates with the help of general information.

What has been said on *market projections* therefore also applies here. The possibilities and usefulness of this device may now be examined more closely.

The knowledge of demand and its probable development is of relatively little importance for the single small producer. To him market prices will be the most important indicator; if they imply a profit he will produce; if they do not, he will have to stop production sooner or later. The quantity of his own production hardly influences the market.

It is otherwise for a larger producer. His supply may very well influence the market and for his investment plans to be well-devised he will want some knowledge about future demand. Accordingly the number of large firms undertaking demand studies of their markets is already considerable and is increasing.

The same is true of production programs of countries as a whole. Even if production is in the hands of relatively small individual producers the total of their product will often be important in relation to the market as a whole, and expansion beyond what the market can take would mean waste. On the other hand, the extent of the market will depend on the rise in income generally and hence it will be related to the program. As far as internal demand is concerned, it may even be argued that investments should be distributed among the various industries exactly as the increased income is distributed among the various goods demanded. Such an investment program for the home market might be called a *harmonious program.* Demand analysis can make a considerable contribution toward making a program harmonious. It may also help to strengthen confidence in a sustained growth of markets.

Although the international market is less influenced by production increases in any one country, there have nevertheless been numerous instances in which this influence has been marked. This is true particularly of raw materials which are produced in a small number of countries, such as jute, cotton, rubber, coffee, etc. Here, too demand analysis is very useful to the programming country.

Recently considerable progress has been made in the field of econometric demand analysis. Programming agencies may advantageously make use of the results. This type of analysis requires the recruitment of experts or subcontracting with institutes specializing in this field. These are to be found in a number of developed, as well as in underdeveloped, countries. Significant results can, however, now be obtained with the aid of more pedestrian methods. And common sense should, of course, always have the final word.

The *testing of cost estimates* is the most important aspect of the testing of individual projects. Costs vary a good deal more among countries and individual plants than do market developments. A distinction should be made between processes that are more or less the same everywhere and processes very much dependent on the particular factor endowments of the country. For the first category, a number of standard figures are available, such as the investment costs per ton of steel, or per ton of cement, the quantities of coke per ton of pig iron, or of power per ton of aluminum. Still it should not be overlooked that alternative methods are often available, and that the choice to be made in an underdeveloped country does not necessarily coincide with the choice to be made elsewhere.

It is the second category of processes, those depending on factor endowment, that is much more variable. The essential problem for each country is to find out in which fields its comparative advantages lie. As a rule they will be related to geographical factors such as mineral deposits, quality of the soil, climate and transportation facilities. Particular comparative advantages will then show themselves in low costs of certain raw materials and of transportation. In certain cases a particular skill of the population may add to the advantages.

The only really satisfactory method of exploring a country's potentialities would be a systematic collection of the cost figures; this will as a rule not be possible in the short run, but might be kept in mind as a useful piece of research. Any such systematic ascertainment of cost figures implies a thorough technical exploration of production facilities and the collaboration of numerous technical experts. This aspect of the problem falls outside the scope of this report. In this field the role of the politician, the administrator and the general economist is a limited one. The importance of having accurate and many-sided information of this kind should, however, be recognized; to acquire it requires scientific and technical surveying and research in which the government would have to participate financially to a considerable extent.

The data needed on the cost side of an economic analysis relate, first of all, to the cost of producing a unit of the product or groups of products in question. To the extent that there may be differences between the costs of existing plants and of new plants, these differences or, more generally, the distribution of costs among the various enterprises involved should be ascertained. It should also be determined how costs vary with prices of the raw materials, labor and other means of production. This assumes knowledge of the quantities of these means of production used, per unit of product. The degree of detail needed would depend on the degree of detail of the program: if say, only ten industrial groups were singled out, a sub-division of costs for each of these groups would of course be sufficient. A very important further datum would be the capital investment per person employed (cf. Annex v i).

To the extent possible, data on alternative methods of production should be acquired, provided, of course, that such alternatives exist. This is not easily done. The importance of this knowledge will be further explained in Section iv 3.

ii 5   *Avoidance of International Duplication*

The essence of programming is the avoidance of inconsistencies. One evidence of this, already noted, is the devising of a harmonious program as far as home markets are concerned. Expansion of exports should likewise be based on demand analysis, in this case for foreign markets. There might be still a danger of inconsistencies if two or more countries independently planned to expand the same line of production. Such unco-ordinated programs might result in over-production. Therefore it is desirable that duplication be avoided.

Sometimes bilateral contacts will be sufficient to avoid duplication in its most pronounced form. Although in principle it is a time-consuming procedure and rather haphazard, often it will be the most practical course to take. The arguments given in favor of programming do not end at national borders. Programming ought to be coordinated internationally. Without such coordination other types of duplication also occur, as for example, duplication in analysis. It is not very efficient for sixty countries all to be studying world market development to some extent. They had much better use as their basic data the results of a few centralized studies. These studies should bear on the probable development of world markets and some of their determinants. The estimates should be based on a number of explicit assumptions as to population, productivity, weather conditions, general policy, etc., and possibly certain alternatives should also be presented. The studies might be undertaken by existing international agencies; in fact, they are already being made in some fields.

There should not be a monopoly in this field; much benefit may be derived from sound criticism and discussion.

II 6   *Types of Programming to be Applied Under Varying Circumstances*

The question may now be put to what extent the programming techniques to be applied must depend on the particular circumstances of each case. Although there is probably less need for differences in approach than is sometimes believed, it cannot be denied that the emphasis must sometimes be shifted from one element of programming to another, and that the outcome of the planning process is necessarily dependent on the characteristics of the given situation.

In what follows, some of these characteristics together with consequences for the program are illustrated.

1. Probably the most important factor is the *stage of development* a country has reached. In the earlier stages of development, the historical record will not provide much of a glimpse of future possibilities; the most important lines of production may still have to be determined and established and probably there is need, first of all, for some general facilities for which public investment is required. Detailed programming at this stage would hardly be appropriate, but a rough idea of the rate of development and the most characteristic comparative cost advantages of the country will be necessary. In the later stages, on the other hand, the probable course of development will be more clearly discernible and more diversified action

will be called for, distributed over more sectors and based on a more detailed type of programming. Accordingly, the content of the program will be different. In the early stages data on the costs and external markets of potential products will be important and those on the development of the internal market and its compartments of less significance. In the later stages a more precise study of internal demand becomes useful. The appraisal of some public investment projects will be very important in the early stages, while an effort to stimulate private projects in manufacturing industry should be postponed to a later period. It may even be simpler, in making the programming estimates, to start with the cost side, rather than with the demand side.

2. Another important feature of the economy is the degree of activity and initiative in the private sector. Where the private sector is rather passive, either more initiative must originate in the public sector, or other types of stimulation must be provided.

3. The type of programming needed will also depend to some extent on the particular *bottlenecks* with which the country is faced. They may either be general or specific in nature. The most important examples of the former are capital scarcity and scarcity of foreign currency. If *capital* is the bottleneck, every care must be taken to assure its most effective use. The supply of capital will be decisive for the rate of development found to be possible; preference will have to be given to labor-intensive activities and measures will have to be taken to induce investors to follow this preference. Such a situation contrasts with that prevailing in a country like Iraq, where there is now a surplus of capital and where other factors will therefore be decisive.

Another general bottle neck may be *foreign exchange,* and here exports take the key position. A distinction may again be made between situations in which exports are limited in variety and those in which they are diversified. If only one or a few products are decisive, the furtherance of these products ranks high in policy determination, and accordingly a correct analysis of the prospects for these products is of primary importance in programming.

Bottle necks of a more specific character are exemplified by a *transportation* bottle neck. In such cases, a road building program or the construction of harbor facilities would seem to be among the more urgent projects. Other examples are a scarcity of certain types of *skilled labor*, calling for training measures, or local scarcities of *dwellings*, requiring a building program.

4. A fourth important influence on the character of programming is to be found in the *general attitude of the people* with regard to government measures: the degree of public spiritedness and the willingness to cooperate, and in the quality of administration. Under favorable conditions more elaborate measures may be taken to further development in the private sector. Accordingly, more detailed research may perhaps then be appropriate. Thus it is conceivable that subsidies might be paid for employing workers in order to stimulate labor-intensive activities. This is possible only if the purpose of such a measure is understood and if the management of the enterprises and the administration of taxes is sufficiently reliable to permit this rather subtle type of regulation.

5. Finally, another factor which will necessarily influence the programming technique is the *quality and nature of the data available.* This will not usually be completely independent of the stage of development or the general level of education, but nevertheless it may vary as between countries otherwise comparable. Clearly there is less scope for the making of refined calculations if the data available are poor than if they are reliable and abundant. Nevertheless, there is a tendency to over-emphasize the influence of the quality of data on the type of programming required. More guesswork is needed if the data are poor, but the logic of programming is not necessarily different.

The same statement applies to the influence of circumstances as a whole on programming. While it is true, that as just indicated, there is some such influence, it should not be forgotten that the basic logic of the development process is not different. It is the relative size of the sectors and their increase in time, and the relative importance of the instruments of policy, which vary and thereby change the practical appearance of the problems, but the core of programming, the attempt to arrive at a consistent picture of potentialities and desirabilities, does not change; neither do the fundamental relations between the main economic phenomena.

CHAPTER III Appraisal of Projects;
Public Investment

III I *Need for a Uniform Method of Determining Priorities*

The lack of complete information about all possible projects that may open up advantageous lines of production constitutes, as we have seen, a handicap either to selecting the best projects to be undertaken by government or to inducing private interests to do so. Only projects which are known to private or public investors can be elements of the pattern or program, and it may be that some unknown projects would have been better than some of those chosen. General programming offers a safeguard against such errors, though only a partial one. From it certain general criteria by which to appraise individual projects may be derived. They should fit into the general program. A frequent handicap to selection of the best projects is a lack of uniformity in the criteria applied by the various ministries of the administration or even by the various services and bureaus of a single ministry. This lack may be due to political decisions in the past; or to some preconceived ideas about one type of investment; or to a particularly strong personality among the administrators. It may result in an unjustified preponderance of certain types of projects or preference to certain individual projects. Some countries subsidize agricultural investments, directly or indirectly, for reasons of security. Others think that heavy industries are particularly important for their prestige. Often public investments are not selected sufficiently critically. Sometimes it happens that a new government does not even complete the projects begun by its predecessor.

All this means waste. And it calls for a uniform method of appraising the projects presented by the various agencies of an administration, whether public or private, industrial, agricultural or commercial, "productive" or "unproductive." To be sure, a completely uniform appraisal will be almost impossible, especially as far as the unmeasurable aspects are concerned. To compare the advantages of an electricity plant with those of a hospital or a school will always be difficult, but at least it can be made clear what increase in material production is sacrificed if a school or hospital is built. A final choice will always have be made, on the basis of all information and on certain subjective valuations, by those who are politically responsible at the highest level. Uniformity can be aimed at only for the measurable aspects; and the results of such an appraisal will have to be taken into account by the policy-makers as one item of information, together with other information, but as a very important item.

To arrive at a satisfactory method of appraisal, one should, first of all, have in mind that investment policy is part of the general policy of the government and that the selection of investment projects cannot be divorced from other decisions. It is the combination of decisions which must be the most efficient avenue to the goal set. This applies in particular to the important realm of tax policy, already discussed, which has an immediate bearing on private investment. Tax policy should be such as to induce private investors to play a part in the general development program. (cf. Section IV 4.)

At the same time, the investment program must fit into the production program for the country as a whole, as estimated by the method of general programming (Chapter II). It should not demand more resources than can possibly be made available, taking account of existing commitments because of works in progress.

Finally, the program should be composed of such projects as would make the maximum contribution to the country's welfare, present and future. The techniques by which these objectives can be achieved, more or less, will now be described. The test to be applied may in a general way be called the *national welfare test;* if welfare is defined to mean production or consumption, we may also speak of the *national product or consumption test.*

The application of a test for selecting projects does not suggest what measures should be taken to assure that the projects will actually be carried out. These measures are discussed in Chapter IV.

III 2   *Simple Methods Sometimes Applicable*

The methods to be discussed in this chapter are, as a rule, rather laborious and any feasible simplification would be welcome. There appear to be some such simplifications; one type is here discussed.

Their basis is to be found in the phenomenon of *complementarity.* Certain facilities will be found necessary because they perform auxiliary functions for more primary objectives. The construction of a road requires provision for its maintenance. The construction of an industrial plant in a remote region requires the construction of a number of dwellings; and certain communications facilities. Once it has been decided to carry out the main projects, the execution of the auxiliary activities has also to be accepted.

Perhaps the most important general examples of this principle are to be found in investments in *transportation* facilities and in *power* plants. Both transportation and power are needed in almost every type of production. This probably explains why, as a rule of thumb, derived from past experience, investments in transport facilities are a fairly constant proportion of total investment, amounting to about 20-25 per cent. This applies to countries of differing structure and to periods of different "prime movers" of development: it applies to the era of railway construction as well as to the era of industrial development. Some pertinent data will be found in Annex v 4.

Power production, too, has to keep pace with general production, or more particularly with industrial production as a whole; and accordingly the appraisal of power plants can be based on a proper demand analysis. In economic terms this procedure may be defined by pointing to the low elasticity of demand for power. Nevertheless, although this may be true as a rule, it is not always so and the limits of this complementarity should be kept clearly in mind. In some cases an alternative method of production, requiring less power, may be feasible; and it may well be that in underdeveloped countries a saving on such a capital-intensive item may be very important. Power requirements of individual industries should not, therefore, be calculated on the basis of figures for similar industries in other countries, but should be examined with the object of taking the most appropriate choice among technologies (cf. Section IV 3).

There are other possible applications of the complementarity test, even where elasticity is in principle higher. *Public health* facilities offer an example. It is not advisable to apply standards in this field out of line with the general level of welfare. It may well be that the population would rather have more food than certain refinements in the medical sphere. Some reflection of the people's free choice should be preserved, even where the general public interest is paramount.

Thus, although the complementarity test may therefore be of some help in certain well-defined cases, its applicability should not be exaggerated. For a country as a whole, complementarity may apply to transportation and to power investments. For regions to be developed, it will not always be appropriate or possible to apply the test. Or rather, the activities to which transportation facilities and power are complementary cannot themselves be accurately foreseen: total production of the region may still be a highly uncertain entity. This sometimes is the very reason why private investment in transportation and power is not forthcoming and why public investment is the only practical possibility.

III 3 *Consequences of Projects*

For a complete national welfare or product test to be applied, the first type of data required has to do with the consequences of each project. What additions to national product can be expected? What changes in other aspects of welfare are probable? What additional costs are involved? The answers to these questions first of all require a detailed technical description of the project. This will not be discussed here, since it falls outside the scope of an economic report. For the consequences to be correctly imputed, some economic analysis will also be necessary, however, since there are consequences not immediately visible to the technician. These have sometimes been described as the *indirect* and the *secondary consequences.*

Indirect consequences are those to be expected in the absence of further changes in total national income. They are the adjustments on the supply side required by the projects, and as a rule they will be found in the stages of production vertically related to the new production, i.e., the stages preceding or succeeding the process involved.

Let us consider a project of land reclamation, which will enable a certain region to produce more sugar cane. An indirect consequence of producing more sugar cane may be that more raw sugar will be produced; a second that more refined sugar will be produced; a third, that more refined sugar will be distributed. Should the increased production at each of these stages of industry and trade be ascribed to the land reclamation project? That depends on the circumstances. If there is idle capacity to produce raw sugar from the cane, it is correct to attribute the increased raw sugar production to the reclamation scheme; if there is no such idle capacity, it is not correct. If the country concerned has been importing raw sugar to supplement its own production and refining it, then the refining process should not be imputed to the reclamation scheme. And so on. It should be clear from the foregoing that a careful comparison is needed of (i) the situation created by the execution of the project, and (ii) the situation that would have existed had the project not been undertaken. For a determination of the consequences, there is required a definite knowledge, or rather estimate, of the development of the economy as a whole. This is why programming must play its part in the procedure.

This statement should, however, be interpreted in a practical way. Too great a degree of perfectionism should be avoided. It is more the approach which matters than every conceivable detail, and above a certain limit the better is the enemy of the good. Sometimes the indirect consequences need not be calculated separately but can be included in the calculation of so-called "accounting prices" (cf. Section III 6).

Secondary consequences consist of the changes in production which are the consequence of the change in national income, both in the short and the longer run, connected with the new production. Such changes do not always occur; in particular they will not if productive factors are already fully employed, even without the new production.

In underdeveloped countries this is often not so, however, and there is therefore a case for considering secondary consequences. It may be, however, that the estimate of secondary consequences must be rough, and that it can be arrived at only by the addition of a figure proportional to income created directly and indirectly (i.e., to primary income derived from the project). In such circumstances the appraisal of projects may also be based on their primary effects only. A more refined—if still rough—estimate of secondary consequences may be made if the proposed project is likely to influence general economic development, e.g., through its effect on savings. This may be the case where the choice is as between a capital-intensive and a labor-intensive project: much less may be saved out of incomes created by the latter, than by the former. Another example of secondary consequences is the influence which may be exerted on government investments because subsidies are needed (cf. Section IV 4).

III 4 *The Use of Scarce Factors*

The choice of certain projects, together forming a program, out of a larger number of available projects must meet certain conditions. That is to say, not every combination of projects can be eligible. This is also true of the investment "pattern" for the country at large, including private investment.

The most important conditions have to do with the *availability of scarce resources*. By *scarce resources* are meant those factors which are indispensable for the program's execution and which are available in limited quantities only. The most obvious example is of course the availability of capital. For the public sector, the total of (i) government revenue after current expenditure, (ii) domestic borrowing, (iii) admissible deficit financing, and (iv) foreign assistance, represents the upper limit of investment. The program cannot go beyond this limit; at the same time it would be unwise not to use, to the fullest extent, the means available. For private and public investment together similar limits can be indicated.

Capital is not the only scarce factor. Land and a number of types of skilled labor, from leaders down to trained workers, are likewise in this category. The investment pattern should be such as to preserve a sufficient quantity of these factors for the consuming sector, and the economy as a whole should, as far as possible, make use of exactly the quantities available. A final example of a factor which is scarce as a general rule, is foreign currency.

For a desirable long-term program, the conditions set by each of these scarce factors are themselves multiple in character. They must be satisfied to a greater or lesser extent in each of a succession of years and in each of a number of regions. This is usually considered the essence of "planning"; the solution of a jig-saw puzzle of considerable complexity. With more or less standard requirements of capital, man-power and foreign exchange by the larger projects, it will be very useful to have available the blueprints of a large number of smaller projects that may fill the lacunae between the big projects.

The elaboration of a stock of blueprints appears to be a useful tool to this end.

Trial and error may be the method employed to find a program which satisfies these conditions. In certain circumstances, this may be a very cumbersome method. It may be simplified by a technique called "the use of accounting prices." Some aspects of this technique are discussed in the next few sections; further details are given in Annex v 3.

III 5   *Ultimate Aims Pursued*

The conditions set forth in the preceding section do not by themselves define the choice of the projects and their succession in time. It is here that the "test" method has to come in and the criterion for selecting projects has to be applied. The criterion should follow, as will be clear, from the general aims of the government's policy.

The general principle to be followed should be to maximize the contribution of the investment program to the country's well-being. "Well-being" may be taken to mean national income, present and future, with possible corrections for its distribution over social groups or regions. Since these corrections will have to be incidental in most cases, not much can be said about them in a general way. One might conceive of giving a greater "weight" to certain types of incomes, assuming that the marginal value of money is higher for certain income types than for others.

Leaving this for what it is, we will concentrate on the aim of attaining a maximum national product or income, present and future. Alternatively, in order to exclude double counting, we will take a maximum volume of consumption. This in fact excludes double counting, since investment, the other part of national product, is not an end in itself, but meant to increase future consumption. Such a maximum of product or of consumption can only be based on a certain method of comparing future with present values. In order to do so, we have to choose a certain rate of interest to be applied in the calculations.

It is essential that the maximum refers to total national income, i.e., income to be derived from the programmed sectors as well as from the other sectors. This implies that it is not a matter of indifference whether e.g., a project is chosen which leads to higher savings or one (yielding the same contribution to national income) leading to lower savings. The latter project probably will somewhat depress development in the other sectors, as compared with the former. An interesting example may be the choice between a large industrial plant and a set of cottage industry projects. Both projects may produce the same commodity, say textiles, in the latter case by employing many more workers, who do not save, in the former by employing managers and technicians who do.

When stressing the relevance of total income to be obtained, we also intend to point to the difference that may exist between an appraisal based on private profitability and an appraisal based on a national product or national consumption test.

Private profits may be a misleading indicator. In many cases they will underestimate the contribution to be made; also, other incomes will, as a rule, rise. Thus the income of workers, formerly unemployed, may also rise; this is not included in the private profit calculation. A well-known extreme case is the one of highway construction. Unless a toll is charged for use of the highway, no income at all will be derived by the investors and yet the increase in national product may be considerable. In some cases, on the other hand, private profits will overestimate the advantages to be obtained. For the profits may be gained at the expense of incomes of other enterprises, especially of competitors. Profits may be an inaccurate yardstick in other respects: they may be based on prices that do not correctly reflect the value of the factors used or of the products.

This too may be exemplified by the choice between a large industrial plant and a set of cottage industries. Let us assume that for the latter project, four times as many workers are needed to produce the same quantity of textiles as for the former. In the private profit calculation a wage bill will be an item; for the cottage industry project, it will be four times as great as for the large plant. This may well be so high as to preclude any profit. The employment of four times as many workers means a high sacrifice to the employer, since he has to pay the market wage rate. To the country, the sacrifice is much less; it is to be measured by the loss of national product due to the employment of these workers. If the workers have to be withdrawn from other activities this loss is equal to what they would otherwise have produced. But a considerable number of them would have been idle and therefore would have produced nothing. The intrinsic value to the country of a man who would otherwise have been unemployed is very low. And the relevant appraisal of the cottage industry project must be based on these intrinsic values, or, as they will be called, *accounting* prices rather than market prices.

There are other costs which are not always "correctly" calculated by the private investor, i.e., correctly from the nation's point of view. If the official rate of exchange of the country is lower than the intrinsic value of foreign currency to the country, the costs of imports or the proceeds of exports will also be underestimated. This leads to a too favorable calculation for projects with an import surplus and to a too unfavorable calculation for projects with an export surplus.

For various reasons, therefore, it is in the country's interest to base its appraisal of investment projects on independent or at least revised "tests," considering all the consequences of the projects and applying accounting prices.

The outcome of such tests may be used as an immediate basis for action in the field of public investment projects. In the case of private projects investors will, of course, base their decisions on the outcome of their private calculations.

III 6   *The Case for "Accounting Prices"*

In the preceding section the concept of accounting prices has twice been alluded to. Since it is going to play an important role in what follows, it will have to be considered in more detail now. The central point to be made is that a number of market prices, particularly those of the "factors of production" (capital, labor, foreign exchange) often diverge from the "intrinsic value" or "accounting prices" that would prevail if (i) the investment pattern under discussion were actually carried out, and (ii) equilibrium existed on the markets just mentioned. In other words, there are two reasons why market prices do not truly reflect "intrinsic values." First, the realization of the investment pattern will itself influence these values, but only after some time, since investment processes are essentially time-consuming. Secondly, there do exist, in underdeveloped countries especially, a number of "fundamental disequilibria." The most important one is the widespread unemployment—open and disguised. A recent estimate for India runs into several tens of millions. The basic reason in all probability is the lack of complementary means of production, i.e., land and capital. Very probably the equilibrium level of wage rates will be considerably less than market wages. On the other hand, equilibrium interest rates probably are much higher than market rates. Some indication of equilibrium interest rates may be derived from (a) the rates at which it would be possible to attract additional capital and (b) the profitability of marginal projects, corrected for risks involved (such as inflation risks). Even if it is difficult to obtain figures of any accuracy, it would be wise to try figures of the order of 10 per cent and over, if only to observe the consequences. As an illustration it may be recalled that in the middle of the 19th century, the long-term bond yield in the United States was 7% to 8% and that similar rates now prevail in a country like Finland.

In a number of countries there is, in addition, a fundamental disequilibrium in the balance of payments only too well-known, and which it would be rash to ascribe to financial mismanagement only. Here again market rates are different from equilibrium rates.

From this closer consideration of the role to be played by the accounting prices, it may be understood that these prices are the technical instruments to assure the full use, and no more than the full use, of the scarce factors of production available. This indeed is the sense of the phrase "intrinsic value" used to clarify their meaning. They are the prices at which supply is just sufficient to satisfy demand; they represent the value of the marginal product to be obtained with their aid, since projects showing no surplus above the cost, at accounting prices, of the factors used, will be on the margin between acceptance and rejection.

The question may be asked whether it would not be more natural to let market prices find their equilibrium—perhaps by a better economic policy generally—than to apply such artificial concepts as accounting prices and to make the appraisal of investment projects "unduly" complicated. The answer should be that this may be possible for a few markets, such as the foreign exchange market, but that for the others it is impossible. The shifts in intrinsic values to be expected from the realization of the investment pattern, by their very nature, will only take place after the investment is completed, and the fundamental equilibria can be helped only by a prolonged process of investment. Making wages equal to their intrinsic value would mean imposing on the workers a level substantially lower than presently prevails and having the revolution right now.

We have to accept, therefore, that in a number of underdeveloped countries the market price structure is not the correct guide for taking decisions. Some of the implications are considered in Annex v 2, where the consequences as a whole are described.

It will not always be possible, or even desirable, to take the trouble of estimating accounting prices in a more or less exact way. The deviations between market and accounting prices, particularly, due to the first cause—the realization of the investment pattern—may be difficult to ascertain. It may be quite sufficient to make a rough

guess as to the consequences of the second cause, fundamental disequilibrium. Since these consequences are, within certain limits,
independent of the size of the program, the corresponding estimate
may be made once and for all. It is often instructive to consider the
influence exerted on the yield figures by arbitrary changes in accounting prices.

An important practical question is how the realization of the
investment pattern can be assured along the lines desired on the
basis of the accounting price test. Briefly, the answer is that government agencies are within certain limits free to decide to make an
investment even if it does not pay financially, and that they therefore
can behave as the accounting prices would require them to. The
limits set by their budgets will be discussed in Annex v 3. Private
investors, however, can and will do so only if accounting prices can
be made a reality to them. This may be done by certain types of
subsidy and certain types of taxing, tending to stimulate the use of
abundant, and to discourage use of scarce, factors. These measures
are discussed in Section iv 4.

iii 7   *National Product (or Consumption) Test*

The procedure recommended may now be summarized. As has
been explained in the preceding sections, the national product (or
consumption) test of a certain investment project is a calculation of
the contribution of that project to present and future national product or consumption.

The calculation must be based on an accurate assessment of the
project's consequences, estimated for each of a succession of years, as
to value of production and costs. This assessment should include
direct as well as indirect consequences and possibly secondary ones.

Values of production as well as costs should be computed on the
basis of accounting prices, as to which general instructions should
be issued. In countries or regions with structural unemployment,

an accounting price for unskilled labor considerably lower than market wages should be applied. In countries with structural balance of payments difficulties, an accounting exchange rate expressing the intrinsic value of foreign currency should be applied.

The interest rate to be applied should express the real scarcity of capital, to be derived from the marginal yield of projects as well as from marginal rates to be paid for foreign loans.

For practical purposes a procedure may be recommended under which accounting prices are fixed independently of the size of the "pattern" and only reflect the fundamental disequilibrium. Here the projects may be appraised one by one and only those showing a positive contribution to national product would be eligible to be undertaken. The national product test may be corrected for certain effects on income distribution and other elements of welfare not implied in total income, and then be called the national welfare test.

In its most accurate form the test would require a process of trial-and-error with different sets of accounting prices, until a pattern is singled out which would make use of whatever scarce factors are available each year and no more, and which, out of the group of similar programs, would make the greatest contribution to national product. This implies that accounting prices are themselves dependent on the size of the "pattern," and is a very complicated process.

III 8   *Examples of Application*

The application of the national product test, or of the national consumption test, is still in its beginning. It is difficult to give a precise account of this application, since, on the one hand, there is no sharp borderline between the private profit test and the "ideal" national welfare test, and on the other hand, the application of these tests is not always published. As to the first point, it may be observed that there is a whole range of different tests; some public investments will be appraised on the basis of purely private profit calculations; for others, only a few elements of the national product test will be introduced; in still other cases, more and more of these elements will be found. In judging road projects, for example, the advantages for production and income in other sectors of the economy will as a rule be considered; the application of accounting prices of course represents the most difficult element of the complete test. As we tried to make clear, the mere application of accounting wage and interest rates may, however, be very important to underdeveloped countries and some reasonable guesses can be made about these accounting rates. Even if such guesses are too difficult it still seems possible to try a few alternative values if only to establish that the net advantages of some projects are heavily dependent on the level of accounting prices applied, while others are not. This might be exemplified by some figures from Netherlands' investment projects. The reclamation of the newest "polder" in the Zuiderzee project appears to leave only a very modest surplus if market rates are applied and a considerable one if accounting wage rates of 80% of market rates are used (cf. iii 8 Table 1).

The conclusion to be drawn from these figures is that the execution of this project is more attractive during a period of unemployment than during a normal period.

There may be reasons to make a distinction between labor applied during the investment period and labor applied during the period of operation: they are not the same type of labor. One type may be abundant and the other not. Accordingly, many variations are possible, depending on the situation in which the country finds itself.

Another set of figures may be quoted from a road project in the Netherlands (cf. iii 8 Table 2).

Income to be derived from this project has been presented, to a large extent, as savings on imports and on wages. This has to be interpreted, for the nation as a whole, as a possibility of applying to other production the labor saved by taking a shorter road. The

III   8   TABLE 1   Capitalized Income and Costs of "East Polder" [1] (fl. mln.)

	Normal wage rate	Accounting wage rate = 0.8 normal
Income:		
Home sales	1734	1734
Additional exports	1699	1699
	3433	3433
Costs:		
Imports	745	745
Interest	170	170
Government services	137	137
Wages	1769	1425
Entrepreneural income	578	462
Total	3399	2929
Surplus	34	504

[1] These figures are provisional only and have no official status.

III   8   TABLE 2   Income and Costs of a Road Project in the Netherlands (Units: 1000 glds.)

Line	Accounting Prices (in % of market prices)				
Imports	100	130	100	130	130
Wages	100	100	75	75	50
1. *Income*	988	1029	825	866	703
2. Import saving	138	179	138	179	179
3. Wages saved	652	652	489	489	326
4. Other	198	198	198	198	198
5. *Costs*	378	397	329	338	280
6. Imports	64	83	64	83	83
7. Wages	234	234	175	175	117
8. Other	80	80	80	80	80
9. Income/Cost	2.61	2.59	2.59	2.56	2.51

value to be attached to such labor saving will depend on the situation of the labor market. The proportion of wages to imports appeared to be roughly the same on the income side and on the cost side, with the consequence that relative surplus hardly changed with the application of accounting prices for either wages or foreign currency. Since surpluses in addition were quite considerable, these projects could be recommended under all circumstances.

The test seems particularly appropriate for the selection of projects to be postponed in periods of inflation or of projects to be accelerated or started in slack periods. Even if the test has already been applied it may be useful to assure that application is uniform. It sometimes happens that one government department applies a test taking account of secondary consequences to a considerable extent while other departments do not. Or it may be that secondary consequences are calculated in a period of full employment, when they will clearly not occur.

CHAPTER IV   Methods by which to

Explore, Appraise and Stimulate

Private Investment

IV   I   *The Search for Sound Projects*

A large portion of government investment projects relates to activities of a general character, such as transportation, power or education, needed in almost all sectors of economic life and only partly dependent on the specific products of the country. Private projects are to a much greater extent directed towards the production of specific goods; and it is of primary importance to the economy as a whole that they be directed toward the correct products. Often not very much is known about the comparative cost advantages of a country; private firms can hardly do more than make cost estimates for a few products in which they are interested.

As already observed, we are here faced with the most difficult problem of development policy: the search for sound projects. Government agencies will not, as a rule, be able to solve this problem by themselves. They may, by their general policy, as we observed in Chapter I, stimulate and give some guidance to the private investor. That general policy will be discussed in this chapter.

In the search for sound projects an attempt may be made to study the country's possibilities in a more systematic way, by making a general survey of national resources: a description of the qualities of the soil in the various regions of the country, of the mineral de-

posits and of the skills of the population. On the basis of such a
survey rough estimates of the costs of production for the most promising goods may be attempted; and these provisional estimates may
be the basis for more accurate computations by private firms. It
would seem appropriate for government agencies or university institutes to make the survey and the rough cost estimates. But usually
decisions must be taken in the absence of such a survey.

IV 2   *Role to be Played by Market and Cost Analysis:*
          the Choice of Industries

The more refined estimates on which private investment projects
have to be based should not rest only on the technological data
which they usually take as their starting point. They should also
pay attention to the economic ties with the outer world. Especially
if large projects are under consideration, their influence on the
economic situation and hence on some of the economic "data" for
the project should not be overlooked.

As already discussed in Sections II 3 and III 4, the general development program of the country might be the starting point. If such
a program does not exist, some sort of a substitute for it might be
taken. This implies, among other things, that investors should have
in mind the normal expansion of demand, as well as the probable
course of prices, wages, etc. Even if the private investor need not
bother too much about such questions, they should be the government's concern. The function of this analysis of the economic background of the projects is to ascertain that they fit more or less into
the general development.

On the other hand, there may sometimes be reasons to revise the
general development plan on the basis of data from a specific project.
This may be so particularly if the cost level of a certain product
appears to be out of line, either favorably or unfavorably, with what
was originally expected. It may be that the cost estimates disclose

unexpected possibilities—mostly as a consequence of mineral deposits or of better transportation facilities than were originally anticipated—or it may be that unexpected difficulties arise. In matters of cost analysis particularly, the private investment project is able to supply the more relevant information, whereas in matters of market analysis the general program may be the safer background. This illustrates the way in which market and cost analysis have to cooperate, not only in order to arrive at a more precise general program, but also to arrive at better individual projects.

The question which industries—in the broadest sense of this word—a country should select for its development may now be answered somewhat more explicitly. It is impossible to be very specific here; the question only makes sense if the context of a particular country is given. Even then there are no fool-proof recipes available. From the preceding discussion it will be clear that the following elements have a role to play in this choice.

First, the special agricultural and mineral products suitable to the soil and the climate must be determined.

Secondly, the products favored by the transportation facilities of the country have to be considered. Water transportation will often facilitate, for example, the supply of relatively heavy raw materials produced not too far away. Both categories of these products should be viewed broadly: the study should cover not only to what extent the raw materials or semi-finished products, but also the final products, can be advantageously produced in the country.

Thirdly, attention should be given to the development of home demand as a consequence of rising incomes. Of course, not necessarily all home demand will best be satisfied by home production, but the latter generally has transportation advantages as compared with imported products. This applies to goods with high transportation costs in particular, and still more to services that have to be rendered on the spot. A systematic investigation as to the probable development of this demand may therefore be helpful.

Finally, in countries with considerable unemployment, a preference should be given to labor-intensive industries, as has already been explained. This point will be considered more closely in the next section.

IV 3   *Choice of Technology*

A matter of peculiar importance is the choice of technology. To a large extent this choice will be determined by physical conditions in the broadest sense: the character of the soil or of the raw materials, the nature of transportation facilities, etc. Often there will hardly be a real choice.

Nevertheless, there are a number of industries in which a variety of technical methods are available. And there is one aspect of this choice that is of basic importance to the economy of the country: the aspect of capital intensity. Most underdeveloped countries are countries of extreme scarcity of capital. The position of capital is completely different from what it is in developed countries; and it is the necessary corollary of the position of labor, i.e., of human beings. The desperate situation of large parts of the population may be said to be due to lack of capital. Even a small waste of capital may bar the possibility of improving the situation of superfluous labor. The utmost care in choosing technologies is therefore needed; everything should be done to restrict capital requirements for a given type of production.

There are reasons to suspect that the correct choice is not always made. One reason is the tendency to copy technologies from developed countries: many technicians consider "advanced technologies" as something desirable by itself. They base this preference in part, perhaps, on higher technical perfection of the product to be obtained. Since their responsibilities are very limited, they often fail to see the social consequences of their choice: less employment than would otherwise have been possible. So it may be advisable for countries

short of capital not to use one-man street cars or not to mechanize
road construction or road maintenance.

Another related reason is that decisions are taken on an incorrect
basis of calculation. Even those who understand that it is not necessarily the most advanced technology, but the cheapest, which should
be selected, make mistakes in their computations as to what is the
cheapest method. Obviously the cost of labor should be compared
with the cost of capital; "cost" to be interpreted as "cost to the nation." Here the problems discussed earlier arise again. Market
wages will as a rule be higher than accounting wages; and interest
rates charged by international institutions may be lower than the
accounting rate discussed in Section III 6. Both deviations tend to
slant the calculations in the same direction, in favor of too capital-
intensive technologies. A careful and thorough re-appraisal of a
number of projects would seem in order. Where private projects are
involved it is clear that private investors can base their decisions only
on the calculations relevant to their own interests. Here the government may induce them to do "the right thing" by a system of
subventions (cf. Section IV 4).

A final point to be mentioned refers to the choice of the *number
of shifts*. It goes without saying that working in one shift only
means that equipment will be idle for two-thirds of the time. Although social considerations admittedly are involved, working with
two, and sometimes three, shifts has many advantages.

IV 4   *Methods of Stimulating Private Investment*
    A   *Protection, Subventions, Tax Provisions*

For several reasons, discussed above, it seems appropriate, in large
sectors of the economy, to rely on private production and investment. It may happen, however, and it does happen, that private
activity falls short of the most desirable level or is applied in wrong
directions. Development policy therefore should include an elab-

orate system of stimuli and deterrents intended to provide some guidance to private activity. In this and the subsequent sections some of the methods of stimulating investment will be discussed and illustrated.

The most important measures are, of course, to be found in the field of financial policy, where often considerable stimuli can be created. The oldest device is the one of *protecting* against foreign competition the industries which it is desired to develop. The appropriateness of this method has been discussed at length for a long time. The free-trade doctrine asserts that under certain conditions free trade, i.e., the absence of protection, leads to a maximum of world production. On the basis of this argument, and assuming that the particular conditions are met, protection should be rejected.

The conditions are not, however, necessarily always fulfilled. One of the conditions is that the resulting income distribution is accepted as the most desirable one. This also implies accepting the income distribution as among countries as the most desirable one. To the extent that this may be doubted, it is possible to influence that income distribution by the imposition of tariffs. These may affect the terms of trade between countries in such a way as to favor the country applying them by lowering its demand for import products, the country may depress their prices and hence obtain them on better terms. This of course applies only to countries or groups of countries able to exercise a considerable influence on their own import markets. The tariff to be aimed at is referred to in literature as the "optimum tariff."

Another condition on which the free-trade doctrine is based is that productivity is independent of the volume of production and of any opportunity to obtain training and acquire skill. The doubts as to this assumption have led to the acceptance of the so-called *"infant industry argument"* for protection: import duties would be acceptable for an initial period during which a country would gain experience in running a certain industry.

Theoretically an objection against these exceptions could still be made: there appear to be other measures which can do the same job even better than protection. Income distribution among countries might be improved by direct transfers instead of by the indirect and complicated way of tariffs. Such transfers would leave world production at its maximum and hence the world at large better off. Similarly, infant industries might be helped by overhead subsidies rather than import duties. Subsidies on overhead costs do not affect marginal costs and therefore do not distort the price structure and consumer choice, as import duties—if applied unevenly—do. Theoretically, therefore, the best policy still would be free trade, provided that income transfers take place and subsidies are accepted.

For practical purposes, i.e., for purposes which it is difficult to integrate into theory, some recurrences to protection may still be appropriate. On the one hand, the possibility of international income transfers is not a reality, to any large extent, in the present political atmosphere; and on the other hand import duties are sometimes much more easy to administer than subsidies. In certain circumstances even quantitative restrictions may have to be applied as the instrument of protection, as for instance if foreign competitors try to eliminate their infant colleagues by dumping.

Import duties based on the infant industry argument should be *temporary* only. A five-year period is often said to be appropriate, and has been accepted in several international agreements. Governments should determine firmly not to depart from this maxim. After World War II the Netherlands government applied the device of protection to some 20 to 25 new industrial products, most of them metal products. Protection was strictly limited to items that had not been produced in the Netherlands before; the period of protection was three years. In addition it was decided that the maximum percentage of total imports that could be protected in this way would be 2.5 per cent. At present the device is hardly in use because of subsequent international agreements. Two products are still protected and generally speaking the results have been satisfactory. (Cf., however, Section IV 9.)

As already said, *subsidies* may, however, be the better course to follow, certainly if the number of plants involved is small. The well-known arguments in favor of subsidy rather than protection are (i) that subsidy is a more open technique: everybody can observe it; (ii) that there is a safeguard against its being unnecessarily continued: it has to be discussed each year; and (iii) that it need not distort the price structure. The latter argument holds true only if the subsidy takes the form of a lump sum. It is of some importance to the industry concerned itself; with this method of aid the price of the product can be lower than in the case of a "protected" product and demand therefore will be higher. One particular type of subsidy applied for the "distressed areas" in the Netherlands has been a 25 per cent subsidy on building costs, with a specified maximum.

An important and general argument in favor of certain forms of subsidy can be derived from the difference between market prices and accounting prices of certain factors of production, notably labor. In a country with significant structural unemployment, such a subsidy should be equal to the difference between market wage rate and accounting rate, i.e., it may even be of the order of magnitude of market wage rates themselves. Its effect should be to induce employers to revise their profit calculations and to bring them in line with the national interest. The result may be an important saving on capital. Thus it may be that cottage industries would become more attractive than large-scale plants, e.g., in cotton textiles.

Many may doubt the practical possibility of such a far-reaching measure. One of the doubts would be based on budgetary considerations. In fact this measure, if applied to all enterprises, would charge the government budget with enormous amounts that would have to be financed out of taxes. It may be that certain government investments would thus become impossible. To the extent that this applies it should be taken account of as a disadvantage, to be set off against the advantages. Tax revenue, however, would probably rise, since in most industries profits or sales, or both, would rise considerably. On the other hand, the tendency to tax evasion would correspondingly increase. Another point of doubt has to do with the administrative complications. To the extent that enterprises pay taxes, one might conceive of an allowance proportional to wages paid; this would not be particularly difficult to administer.

If an unemployment dole exists and is paid out of public funds, a subsidy equal to the dole would not cause budgetary difficulties. If the subsidy is less than the dole, it has two advantageous results: it stimulates the absorption of unemployed workers and at the same time reduces public expenditure. This measure was applied with considerable success in the Netherlands, during the great depression, for certain types of investment projects, namely, improvements on farms. An extensive account has been published showing that the measure worked to the advantage both of farmers and of public finance.

Subsidies on the employment of unskilled workers may also be made in the form of an *exemption from, or reduction in, social charges,* if such charges exist. There appear therefore to be several possible ways in which this type of subsidy may be applied and in view of the importance to be attached to any reduction of unemployment the choice of a particular method should be given the most careful consideration.

The budgetary consequences might again be lessened if, as a logical counterpart of the subsidy, an *extra charge* were introduced for the *supply of capital.* Loans to be made by the government to either lower authorities, or government enterprises, or even private enterprises, might be made at a rate higher than the moderate rates at which the government itself borrows, on the principle that the accounting price of capital justifies such a differential.

Tax provisions are the third measure in the financial field that may stimulate investment activity. A general and simple form might be a reduction of company taxes. Such a reduction would leave more profits in the hands of entrepreneurs and hence encourage further investment. But the efficiency of this type of tax measure may be doubted. The reduction would apply to everybody and in many cases would stimulate consumption rather than investment.

A more direct link between tax reduction and investment may, however, be introduced: the reduction may be made dependent on proof that certain investments have been made. It may take the form of exempting from taxation certain additional depreciation allowances on new investments. Measures of this kind were adopted in many countries after World War II.

Care should be taken not to create tax privileges for some industries not extended to others. Apart from the outright abuse they may lead to, it is economically wrong to distort the price and cost structure by deliberately selecting industries for tax reductions while leaving others unaffected. This does not rule out, however, tax measures in fact applicable to some industries only, if the basis of such an exception is a general principle. It is conceivable e.g., that subsidies in the form of tax reductions might be given based on the degree of labor intensity (cf. Section IV 3) of an industry.

IV 5. B   *Programming, Information, Encouragement and Demonstration*

Apart from financial support in some way or another, there are other ways to stimulate private investment. These are directed toward facilitating investment, in particular by activities which a central agency can perform more effectively than can individual industrialists.

In view of the great importance of correct information on a number of outside factors, one of the fields where this greater effectiveness can certainly be attained is the field of *information*: information on markets, on official measures, technical information and social information. A distinction may be made between some more sophisticated types of information mixed with scientific research, and simpler information.

The former type may be exemplified by the use to be derived, by private business, from government programming of economic development. Correct forecasts on a firm's expansion possibilities are not easy and, if done well, are rather expensive. The most difficult part for the firm expert is the general aspect of the forecast, which depends on the country's general development, since this in turn depends on a number of factors of government policy. In any case, it would be a tremendous waste of energy if each firm, or even each industry, were to try to make such forecasts. The arguments in favor of some international co-ordination in this type of research apply even more strongly to co-ordination on a national scale (cf. Section III 5). It has been the experience in the Netherlands that there is a growing interest, in managerial circles, in the long-term development programs made up by the Director General of Industrialization and the Central Planning Bureau. In the Netherlands, the producers of equipment for electricity plants did not know what total volume of investment by electricity plants was to be expected in the ten years ahead. Industry and firm economists are making use of the figures in order to have a background for their own more refined demand estimates.

These demand estimates and a number of other analyses—e.g., on organization or on specified cost items—are to an increasing degree also being entrusted to specialized private institutes. In the Netherlands, the Netherlands Economic Institute, affiliated with the Netherlands School of Economics at Rotterdam, specialized in demand analysis for private firms and in the last ten years such analyses have been made for 34 goods or services, distributed as follows:

Food	15
Other raw materials, non-durable consumer goods	3
Raw materials for durable goods	5
Finished investment goods	2
Fuel	3
Services	6

For several of these goods a considerable number of national markets has been analyzed.

The second category of information includes commercial facts and all sorts of administrative regulations. Examples are foreign trade figures of particular countries, split up into a great number of components and arranged in comparative tables relevant to the problem in view; particulars on firms trading in different kinds of materials, machines, etc.: details on import duties and tax regulations in a large number of countries; and so on. This type of information may be supplied by public as well as private agencies. In the Netherlands, and probably elsewhere as well, the Ministry of Economic Affairs has an Economic Intelligence Service which supplies a large amount of such information. In addition, each of the eleven provinces, as well as certain municipalities, have so-called "economic-technological institutes" which supply data of a mixed economic and technological character to enterprises planning to expand their business in a certain region. Together with the Director General of Industrialization and the Central Institute for Industrialization, they work out regional development plans for depressed areas. Further details about this activity are set forth in the next section.

In addition to information, these services have also provided advice on matters of organization, co-operation and marketing. The idea of the "export combination" of a certain number of medium-sized enterprises, of the "combined show" at industrial fairs, of common research on design, packaging and markets and of collective export credit insurance have all been launched by the Information Service of the Ministry of Economic Affairs. This type of *encouragement* of a certain action may also take the form of discussions, on the initiative of a government agency, with representatives of certain branches of activity, regarding unused opportunities. Suppose there is an opportunity to establish a hotel in a region attractive to tourism and the initiative is not forthcoming; it may then be encouraged by such conversations. The Director General of Industrialization in the Netherlands frequently suggested the pos-

sible production of certain parts previously imported and several of
his initiatives were successful.

A final element to be mentioned in this class of measures is the
erection of *demonstration* plants. In the field of agriculture this is
a well-known practice, generally believed to have been successful.
New tools, seeds, fertilizers and methods are demonstrated to the
farmers or experiment farms or in demonstration farms. The idea
has been applied in manufacturing industry as well, e.g., in Vene-
zuela.

IV 6. c   *Financing Facilities: National and Foreign*

Investment has traditionally been financed only partly from the
entrepreneur's own resources, so that credit facilities have always
been an important factor. It is well-known that these facilities are
organized differently in different countries; in some countries special investment banks have long existed, whereas in other countries
they are a new phenomenon. Almost everywhere there is a problem of providing facilities to smaller enterprises, often solved in a
semi-public or co-operative way. Although it is therefore not possible to generalize, it may be said that there is usually in some way
or another a financing "problem." Solutions may be sought both in
the national and in the international field.

In the national field then, the creation of institutes specializing in
medium- and long-term credit for medium- and small-scale enterprises will be useful, if they do not already exist. As a rule they will
have to specialize in terms of a particular type of activity; farm
credit, credit for handicraft, retail trade and manufacturing industry
may be organized separately. Often some government support will
be necessary, in the form either of guarantees or of participation in
the capital resources. To the fullest extent possible, however, the institutions should be concerned with furthering the supply of savings
to these particular channels.

In certain individual cases, especially where large amounts of capital are involved, the usual methods of financing may be impossible. Here government participation may be important. Government participation may range from 100 per cent to a minority interest. There is no reason to consider only the extremes of complete government ownership and completely private ownership. Intermediary forms are even sometimes to be preferred: they may combine the strong points of private and public interest. Much depends on the persons involved and the form of management. Freedom in day-to-day management decisions is very important. On the other hand, the supply of additional capital should not be made an easy matter because of the government affiliation.

Government participation has proved to be successful in the creation of a center of heavy industry in the Netherlands. It was not for doctrinaire reasons that after World War II the central government supplied the capital needed for the erection of a rolling-mill. A certain minimum of steel supply, not exceeding 50 per cent of total consumption, was deemed a necessity for the country's development. The country was willing to import the other 50 per cent from its neighbor countries Belgium and Germany, traditional suppliers of steel. It was deemed preferable that the steel mill be financed privately. Private concerns willing to supply the capital could not, however, be found. It was not a socialist minister who proposed that, in the circumstances, the investment should be made by the state and it was a parliament with less than 30 per cent of socialist members which approved the proposal. The corporation is run very well and has no difficulty maintaining itself in the European Coal and Steel Community.

Another type of government participation in investment may be seen in the same country in the field of agriculture. The new areas reclaimed in what was first the Zuiderzee are government property, and have even been run by government agencies for a short time, because of severe and unknown risks to be expected for the first years. After that period most of the lots are rented to tenants. A small group of farms is, however, operated by state farmers. There is only a slight difference in the operating results of these state farms and comparable private farms.

In view of the scarcity of capital in underdeveloped countries, national resources for financing are limited. Investment of foreign capital is another possibility, which has the additional advantage of sometimes introducing new methods of production.

For understandable reasons there has been much reluctance in some of the underdeveloped countries to admit foreign enterprises, and frequently such enterprises are regarded with suspicion: in the colonial era they often were the symbols of political influence. But this is no longer the case, in many countries, and the situation should be reexamined on both sides. The best thing to be done in the interest of both the underdeveloped areas and the private enterprises concerned seems to be a clear separation of political and economic considerations. Investment of foreign capital from the investor's side, should be treated as a purely economic matter, not influenced by any desire for political activity. Accordingly, economic policies with respect to such investments should be based, by the receiving countries, on their economic significance. Some conditions may be enumerated which seem to be fundamental to a smooth operation of foreign enterprises in underdeveloped countries.

A first set of conditions is that the country's policies with regard to all factors of production should be consistent and clear-cut. The entrepreneur cannot make calculations unless there is a reasonable degree of certainty and of continuity in social legislation, safety requirements, import duties and other trade regulations, taxes and the basic facilities such as the supply of power, transportation and communications. One point of particular interest is the policy with respect to the transfer of dividends to the lending country. In this connection the importance of avoiding violent changes in exchange rates should be stressed.

If more certainty and continuity can gradually be attained in all these matters, an increase in competition will also follow and profits will become more moderate than they are under circumstances of high risks.

Another condition of great importance is that there be a reasonable degree of labor peace. It is remarkable how much the existence of labor peace in the Netherlands after the Second World War has contributed toward attracting foreign enterprises to that country. Labor peace was largely due to the regulations concerning labor conflicts which made government mediation conditional upon terminating the strike or lockout. Such a regulation, in its turn, could work only because the government had the trade union's confidence.

Apart from the conditions just mentioned, the availability of reliable and quick information and a smooth procedure in negotiating are important. Simple though these things may seem, they require exactitude and a co-operative attitude on the part of all concerned.

IV 7. D   *Minor Facilities*

Programming information and credit facilities are only preparatory steps and will have to be followed by the execution of the plans that may emerge. Even if the latter is thought of as essentially a private activity, some help in what might be called minor facilities may be of critical importance. This help would consist of activities to facilitate relationship with the outside world, activities which usually cannot depend on private initiative alone. One example is transportation connections. To set up a plant at a particular site may require the presence of water, road or railway connections. The establishment or improvement of such facilities would be in order. Power and water supplies are of great importance, and they are in part a responsibility of public enterprises. Suitable sites must be made available and they may be prepared by local authorities. Sometimes even the buildings themselves may be turned over to the industrialists. A labor exchange, schools and medical facilities are additional examples of these facilities. It is of quite some importance that a smooth and efficient apparatus be available to overcome the difficulties in these fields. Although each aspect may perhaps be said to be "minor," they are not unimportant as a group. It has in fact been considered the greatest advantage of the developed countries in contrast to the underdeveloped ones that such facilities are, as a rule, already available. This, however is true of the old industrial centers in such countries only and not necessarily to the developing regions. Experience gained in the planned stimulation of private activity in such areas may therefore be of some use to underdeveloped countries as well. As an example the region of South-East Drenthe, in the Netherlands, could be cited. This region, with a rather dense population, formerly made its livelihood from peat digging. With the exhaustion of peat deposits, as well as because of increased competition from coal, the region became a depressed one. The Netherlands government, in co-operation with the province of Drenthe and the municipality of Emmen, worked out a program for development. One of the most important incidents in the course of the endeavors was the decision of A.K.U., the large rayon corporation of the Netherlands, to erect a new plant at Emmen. This decision was undoubtedly influenced to a large extent by the "minor facilities" offered. Certain well-defined additional costs of the investment due to the separation of the plant from the corporation's center (Arnhem) were borne by the government. Road and railway connections were improved and new schools and a hotel were built in Emmen.

The picture would not be complete without mention of a happy coincidence. In the neighborhood of Emmen, in the village of Schoonebeek, mineral oil deposits were discovered during World War II. Their exploitation was postponed until the war was over. At present some 30 per cent of the oil consumption of the Netherlands is produced in that region. These two projects together largely account for the successful recovery of the region.

IV   8   *Public* vs. *Private Activity*

Only when the various measures described in the previous sections do not serve to induce private investors to enter a field generally considered most appropriate for private activity should a different course be envisaged. Such situations may present themselves for various reasons. One such reason may be the absence of sufficient entrepreneurial skill in the population. This is not a hopeful situation, since the development of such skill is a time-consuming process. It has been developed in the older industrialized countries by a process of gradual growth. Industrialists have grown out of handicraft and trade firms, accumulating their skill and knowledge through generations. As is true of every process, this can probably be accelerated. Apprenticeship in older firms inside or outside the country is one way in which this type of training may be organized. Important work for some of the non-profit corporations in the educational field, international and other, seems indicated. As is now generally recognized, the solution to the problem of skills is not primarily a question of university teaching, but rather one of secondary education and free vocational training.

As long as private activity is not, for whatever reason, forthcoming to a sufficient extent, the question arises whether public activity should take its place. This raises a further question often considered fundamental: where should the line between private and public activity be drawn?

It seems useful here not to put things too much in black and white— or should one say black and red? Even in the Soviet Union there is a private sector of peasants, small traders and handicraftsmen, whereas, on the other hand, in the United States, where the belief in private initiative is particularly strong, the public sector is none the less considerable. In most western countries the public sector was much smaller a century ago than it is at present. In nineteenth century Britain the government spent less than 10 per cent of national income; at present, government expenditures exceed 20 per cent in many western economies. The question of the best line of demarcation between the two may perhaps be called the most controversial issue of today's discussion and thinking: it may be said to be the economic side of the clash of doctrines between the communist and the non-communist world.

As might be expected, there is, on both sides of the Iron Curtain, much dogmatic thinking about this issue. The central arguments in favor of public activity in the economic field are that private ownership of capital goods implies the existence of unjustified high incomes to people who do not work and leads to uncoordinated production with consequent crises and unemployment. The central arguments in favor of private activity are that a direct personal interest in the results of production stimulates productivity and avoids the dangers of bureaucracy and abuse of power. Of course a host of further arguments is employed on both sides, but we may confine ourselves to the central ones. The discussion in its essence goes back to the nineteenth century economic discussion between socialists and non-socialists. It has seemed to stagnate since it has been drawn into the ethical sphere, mainly as a consequence of the development of dictatorial governments. The discussion of this form of government raises so many questions on the fundamental issues of life and culture that socio-economic questions have been neglected in the argumentation.

On both sides many of the arguments are therefore antiquated. No account has been taken of recent improvements in both the public sector and in private enterprise, or in mainly state-run economies and mainly privately-run economies. An up-to-date discussion has to be much more refined. And it is of some real importance, since clearly a country living according to some dogmatic belief will in the end be at a disadvantage compared with a country which tries to find the optimum pattern of organization.

Modern experience as well as economic analysis has shown that certain activities can best be undertaken by public authorities, whereas others can best be left to the private sector. Even if it is admitted that a certain centralization is needed in order to avoid crises and waste, important tasks can be left to individuals or private organizations because of higher *internal efficiency*. And even if, on the other side, it is argued that free enterprise automatically leads to a maximum national product, it should not be forgotten that certain general conditions have to be fulfilled before a private economy can operate—here one could speak of *external efficiency,* the efficiency of the relations between productive units—and that it is state activity which has to bring into existence and maintain this framework. These considerations and experience derived from action in particular circumstances have led to the almost general acceptance of certain tasks for the public sector; these are, however, not invariable and depend on a number of characteristic factors. Apart from the well-established task of assuring internal security and performing certain basic juridical functions, the government has, in the economic field, certain tasks briefly referred to in Chapter I:

(i) to create and maintain *healthy monetary conditions;*
(ii) to regulate the degree of activity so as to *avoid mass unemployment;*
(iii) to *correct extreme inequalities* in income distribution; and
(iv) to *supplement private activity* in certain basic fields where for one reason or another that activity falls short of meeting legitimate requirements.

On top of these administrative, supervisory and supplementary tasks there is scope for some *direct participation* of the public sector in production. This is true of sectors so fundamental to the country's existence that direct control is needed, sectors safeguarding the country's security such as a system of flood control and military defense works. It is a question of some subjective judgment whether the country's water and power supply and even parts of its transportation and communications system should not also be included: some countries have answered this question in the affirmative, others have not. Often the development towards government ownership in transportation and public utilities has been a consequence of the imposition of low rates considered to be in the general interest. These low rates have made it difficult to attract private capital and so led to government investments in these facilities.

The argument in favor of some direct government control may also be derived from technical conditions. In sectors showing high fixed costs and economies of scale, free competition will lead to very unstable and often unremunerative prices and there is therefore a tendency for it to be replaced by a monopoly. It is well known that tendencies towards monopolistic combinations in the heavy industries and in railway transportation have their origin in this state of affairs. A private monopoly, however, does not seem attractive for sectors which are fundamental to economic life, and government control of monopolies has been shown not to be an easy matter. Public management may be simpler. Some countries have also considered steel manufacture as belonging to this group. The argument of threatening monopolies might be helpful in splitting up the transportation sector into two sectors, one to which this argument applies and another to which it does not; in the latter category would fall merchandise transportation by motor truck or by inland shipping. Here private management might be preferable, although with certain provisions as to prices.

More important to efficiency than the question of ownership, however, is the question of the *freedom of management.* Where management of public enterprises has freedom in every-day details and administrative control is confined to some broad lines, the internal efficiency of the enterprises appears to be comparable to that of private enterprise with the same quality of management. Some indication of the validity of this comparison is perhaps shown by the Netherlands' experience in the field of coal and steel. As was earlier observed, for half a century Dutch coal mining has been divided about equally between private and state mines. Whatever may be said about the efficiency of the two types, the state mines are not less efficient than the private ones. The Dutch steel industry is practically public property, but it has not the slightest difficulty in competing, in the European Coal and Steel Community, with private steel manufacturers in Germany, Belgium or France.

Interesting experience has also been gained in the field of agriculture. In the newly reclaimed Zuiderzee "polders," a number of farms are state-owned and run by "state farmers." From a comparison of the results of these farms and of comparable private farms in the same area, the tentative conclusion may be drawn that either the state farms are at a slight disadvantage or there is no difference between the two.[1]

One final remark on the subject: the choice need not be a black-or-white choice between wholly public or wholly private ownership. Mixed ownership may sometimes afford a means of combining private efficiency with a desirable direct public control. The device of government guarantees has likewise often proved to be a very useful instrument.

IV 9   *Lessons To Be Learned from Failures*

Not all methods, measures or projects constituting the development policy of a country will in the end prove successful. Economic life is beset with uncertainties and challenges which man has not been able to meet in a completely satisfactory way. Economic history is a history of struggle and of failures as well as successes. But failures are not completely negative since they may teach us what not to do. Some of the lessons to be learned from failures in Dutch development policy may be briefly mentioned here.

As far as *programming* is concerned, the experience so far has been that there is a tendency for statisticians engaged in this type of work

---

[1] The qualification in this statement is due to a technical uncertainty about the nature of one of the cost categories. I am indebted to Dr. A. W. G. Koppejan of the Netherlands Central Planning Bureau for the analysis on which my tentative conclusion is based.

to underestimate the changes that actually take place. Qualitatively this is connected with the continuous occurrence of new factors, mostly technical, but also political or psychological. Quantitatively it may be illustrated by the fact that the average ratio of changes predicted to actual changes was 70 per cent for the Netherlands (and as low as 55 per cent for Scandinavian programs) as far as annual official programming is concerned. Statistical research is continuously being developed and although it would be unreasonable to require a complete coincidence of prediction and reality, some improvement seems possible. Collection of more and better statistics will be the main source of improvement.

Failures in *policy* are often due to the well-known difficulties of lack of understanding of economic problems on the part of politicians, or to pressure exerted by vested interests. It cannot be said that these factors have been particularly strong in the Netherlands in the last ten years and not much can be learned in this respect. The most that can be said would seem to be that there is a certain lack of coherence between the various ministries, due to the responsibility of each minister separately to parliament and due partially also to some skepticism with regard to programming. It may be, however, that this skepticism helped to keep the proper balance between programming and improvisation!

In the particular field of *industrialization* there seem to be a few cases of new enterprises that were not really successful. Their common characteristic is that, although sufficient and even considerable technical skill was available, commercial abilities were insufficient. This phrase, of course, is a catch-all for many different abilities and it is not easy to indicate them all very clearly. Often it is a question of insufficient knowledge about the precise qualities of a product which the market wants or, sometimes, lack of flexibility necessary to follow the changes in demands. Of course there are also failures for which the firms involved can hardly be blamed; bad luck does occur from time to time. One form of bad luck is the attempts sometimes made by foreign competitors to kill the new enterprise by all means of cut-throat competition, especially dumping. In such cases government support may be called for, e.g., by the temporary application of import restrictions.

Not only practical life, but also scientific research, shows many failures; one may learn from them also. The process of scientific development is a continuous succession of new hypotheses or theories being formulated, being refuted upon closer analysis or confrontation with the facts and being amended into a new version. The science of economies is no exception to this rule. It may be said to be in a period of rapid development and the fields of programming and policy design share in this development. It may be hoped that better and more accurate methods will become available in due course. Much will depend on the collection of more and better data bearing particularly on the cost side of production. Whenever possible, attempts should be made to widen knowledge in this field particularly. It should not be forgotten, however, that the role to be played by scientific knowledge and insight in the field of development policy will for a long time to come be only a modest one. The relevant facts of life are too many and too varied to make it possible to reach decisions without a strong intuitive feeling for human relations.

CHAPTER V   Annexes

ANNEX V I   THE CAPITAL COEFFICIENT

Much use has recently been made of the so-called "capital coefficient," a concept not heretofore given a prominent place in economic analysis. As now understood it may be defined as the quantity of capital needed for the production of a unit of product. Since both elements in this definition may be defined in manifold ways, care must be taken in selecting and adhering to a definition.

As to the concept of "product," a choice can be made between value and volume of production (i.e., between money or physical concepts of "product"), and between gross and net product. Capital may, in addition, also be conceived in a more abstract way, and then often will stand for all assets involved in the process of production, or in a more physical way, in which case money or some physical unit may likewise be the yardstick. If physical objects are selected to represent capital, attention must be paid to the difference between the value of a newly established plant and the value of a plant that has been used for some time already and hence is partly worn out. The true measure of capital involved should be the sum total of market value of the equipment and stocks and the depreciation funds accumulated; a fact sometimes neglected. Corrections may be needed for price changes that have meanwhile taken place. (Cf. Annex Table 2.)

Next must be answered the question whether land and other natural resources are meant to be included. Both inclusion and exclusion are possible, and it depends on the problems in question which is to be preferred.

Finally it should at least be realized that skilled labor in a certain sense also contains an element of "capital," in that education and training have been "invested" in the workers.

The use that may be made of the concept of capital coefficient originates in certain technical or statistical facts referring to it. In many individual production processes there exists a fixed proportion between the physical output of products and the quantity of certain means of production, among which are equipment and stocks. With two cars, twice as much freight can be handled as with one car. That is, on the one hand, almost self-evident, but on the other hand it is true given a number of restrictive conditions, only too well known to engineers and economists. This proportionality applies only if no alternative methods of using the equipment are available, as is the case, e.g., in spinning and weaving, where the ratio of equipment to product can be changed by changing the number of workers. Similarly, it can often be changed by varying working hours or number of shifts. To the extent that the constancy applies it is essentially a constancy in the ratio between the quantity of equipment and the gross physical product obtainable. The word "equipment" is now used to indicate the capacity to produce, e.g., the tonnage of ships available, whether new or old (provided they are of the same type).

This individual-industry capital coefficient, essentially a technical concept, may, for the sake of comparison, also be expressed as a ratio of money amounts, but then it is no longer necessary that it be a constant, even if it would be physically a constant. In addition, it varies widely from one industry to another. It is a well-known fact that there are particularly labor-intensive industries as well as particularly capital-intensive ones. Some figures estimated by Professor Leontief illustrate this (see Table 1, page 72).

Instead of using capital-output ratios, one might also use capital per head figures, i.e., the capital needed per person employed in a

ANNEX V I   TABLE I   Capital Coefficients of Some
American Industries

House renting	8.2
Communications	4.6
Railroad transportation	3.3
Medical, education and non-profit organizations	2.7
Agriculture and fisheries	2.5
Coal, gas, electric power	2.2
Metal working machinery	1.2
Iron and steel	1.0
Trade	1.0
Personal and repair service	0.7
Textile mill products	0.5
Motors and generators	0.4
Apparel	0.3
Leather and leather products	0.3
Finance and insurance	0.03

certain activity. These figures are perhaps even more appropriate, since it is the relative factor endowment of a country that should be one of the bases for choosing industries, and for such a selection the capital per head figures are more significant than capital coefficients. Stated in other words: for a given country the number of persons to be employed is known, whereas the quanity of product is not known beforehand but has to be made as high as possible. Some figures of capital per head are to be found in Annex Table 2. It should be stated that these figures are very rough estimates only; for lack of better data census figures have been taken, with a few corrections only.

The remarkable fact should be noted (cf. Annex Table 1) that, as a rule, the products of very capital-intensive as well as only slightly capital-intensive activities are products that do not easily enter into international trade.

Another fact of some importance to development programming is that there may be a marked difference in capital intensity between the activity carried out with a given type of equipment and the activity of producing that equipment. To produce electricity, for example, is a very capital-intensive process; to build an electricity plant, however, is not. The decision to create such a plant therefore implies a decision with respect to two very different kinds of activity.

ANNEX V I   TABLE 2   Capital Per Person Employed (thousands of U.S. dollars, 1950 prices)

Census year	United States 1950	Mexico 1945	India 1950
1. Bread and bakery products	5.0	1.7	3.5
2. Cotton yarn and cloth	8.7	2.1	1.8
3. Flour and grist mill products	39.1	10.4	5.6
4. Iron and steel industries	32.1	10.8	5.7
5. Sugar refining	26.8	8.2	2.6
6. Woodpulp, paper and paper products . . .	10.2	8.9	6.6

Source: Calculations by Netherlands Economic Institute.

Figures are census figures for equipment, machinery, buildings and inventories with three corrections:

(1) figures were derived from equipment value estimates through multiplication by 2 (in order to approach values before depreciation);

(2) they were multiplied by the ratio $\frac{\text{price level of census year}}{\text{price level 10 years earlier}}$ in order to correct for price changes between year of purchase (assumed, on the average to be 10 years earlier) and census year; and

(3) finally, the figures were multiplied by the ratio $\frac{\text{price level 1950}}{\text{price level census year}}$. The first correction was, however, not applied to the U.S. figures, since these are reported to be undepreciated.

Apart from these well-known technical facts on which, nevertheless, much documentation would be very welcome, there is also another statistical fact, only recently discovered. This fact is the relative constancy of the ratio of national capital to net national product. The word "relative" should be kept in mind: the figures so far estimated are subject to wide margins of error and comparison of

any two is possible only within correspondingly still wider margins.
The better formulation, therefore, of the results so far found is that
the variations of the capital coefficient as here defined between
periods as well as between countries is not very systematic. Clearly
the figures depend somewhat on the exact definition of capital.
Some information will be found in Table 3.

ANNEX V I TABLE 3   Capital Coefficients for National
                      Economies

Country	Period	Coefficient	Source
Argentina . . .	1913	5.8	(a)
Australia . . .	1913	5.5	(a)
Italy	1913	4.4	(a)
U.S.A. . . .	1913	4.3	(a)
Japan	1913	3.6	(a)
U.S.A. . . .	1889	3.0	(b)
U.S.A. . . .	1909	3.4	(b)
U.S.A. . . .	1919	3.8	(b)
U.S.A. . . .	1939	3.3	(b)
Average for about 30 countries } . .	Various	4.7 max.[1] 3.0 min.[2]	(c) Derived from re-gression curve on income per head
Mexico . . .	ca. 1955	1.5	(d)
India	ca. 1955	1.5	(d)

[1] For relatively poor countries.
[2] For wealthiest countries.

Sources: (a) Colin Clark, Conditions of Economic Progress (1940), p. 389.
         (b) Simon Kuznets, Income and Wealth of the U.S. (1952), p. 297.
         (c) Colin Clark, Conditions of Economic Progress (1951), p. 503.
         (d) Recent progress reports on economic conditions in the countries con-
             cerned.

The interpretation to be given to these figures clearly is that although technical development has been characterized by an increase
in capital per head, and by an increase in product per head, it so

happens that, for an economy like the United States as a whole, the quantity of product obtained is practically proportional to the quantity of capital. The same result has been found in the case of Great Britain. In addition, the ratio between capital and product seems not to depend on the degree of development of a country. Some of the differences observed seem to be explicable in terms of the factor endowment of the country. (Cf. E. E. Hagen, "Social Accounts and the Incremental Capital-Output Ratio in Underdeveloped Countries," presented at Third Conference of International Association for Research in Income and Wealth, Castelgandolfo, September 1953.) This phenomenon applies to national averages only; it can hardly be expected to apply in an exact way, since as we have already seen, figures for individual activities diverge widely.

For the reasons indicated, the use to be made of the capital coefficient can be one of rough estimation only of the capital needed for a country's development: for a given or desired increase in production the necessary investments can be calculated by multiplication with the coefficient. It is to be hoped that further research will narrow down the margins of error of such calculations which, for the time being, are still considerable.

Given the usefulness of the capital coefficient to development programming for underdeveloped countries, a question of some relevance is whether the coefficient will be higher or lower for these countries than for developed countries. Different opinions have been expressed by different authors. On the one hand the necessity of creating some basic facilities of a very capital-intensive character not yet in existence in underdeveloped countries is an argument for expecting a high coefficient. On the other hand the possibility of developing labor-intensive industries and of improving efficiency by better organization are arguments in the opposite direction. Recent statistical investigations have produced a number of instances in which low coefficients only seemed to prevail: the cases of India and Mexico may be quoted where the coefficient has actually been, in the last few years, as low as 1.5. This may partly be due, however, to particular circumstances. In a recent analysis, one of the reasons for a low coefficient was found to be the introduction of more shifts in heavy industries. Excellent as the measure is, it cannot be repeated once the maximum of shifts has been attained. Good crops may also have played a role. They may be followed by less good crops. The conclusion can only be repeated that further research is of great importance.

ANNEX V 2   FUNDAMENTAL DISEQUILIBRIA
IN UNDERDEVELOPED COUNTRIES
AND ACCOUNTING PRICES

As was briefly indicated in Section III 6, there is reason to believe that most underdeveloped countries are characterized by some "fundamental disequilibria," the most important being that part of the population cannot be gainfully occupied for lack of complementary means of production: land and capital. In certain cases a further disequilibrium, namely one in the balance of payments may occur. Since some rather far-reaching conclusions are drawn from this diagnosis, it seems appropriate to give a fuller picture of what the author supposes the situation to be. This picture, if it is correct, must be consistent and so must the conclusions to be drawn from it.

The point made was that certain prices in these countries do not correctly reflect the intrinsic value of the goods or factors to which they relate. Probably the proceeds of the country's products to the extent sold in the world market do reflect their intrinsic value more or less: more so for products whose contribution to world supply is small, than for products, such as jute in Pakistan, whose contribution is large. The market wage rate, however, probably is higher and the market interest rate lower than their respective intrinsic values. The intrinsic value of labor is so low that wages in accordance with it often would mean starvation. Also the trade unions are able, in a number of cases, to raise wages above what would be an "equilibrium level." This abnormal situation is largely due, in the author's opinion, to the scarcity of capital, and can be ended only by a better balance between population and capital.

With wage rates probably above their intrinsic value, there remains a margin for entrepreneurs which on the one hand is lower than its intrinsic value, but on the other hand is not necessarily low, since market wages are still very moderate. Moreover, the scarcity of entrepreneurs and of capital is so pronounced that their intrinsic value is often extremely high. Profit rates and, as a consequence, interest rates will thus be lower than their intrinsic values; and this fact is strengthened by the circumstance that the interest rates charged by international institutions are usually moderate. Moreover, there is a tendency for underdeveloped countries to organize cheap credit facilities for certain types of small enterprise. All this makes it probable that interest rates on the whole have a downward bias as compared to "accounting rates."

With wages above, and interest rates below, their intrinsic values, there are some further discrepancies in the pricing system. Commodities with a high labor content will be overvalued; commodities with a high capital content, such as, e.g., transport and power rates will be undervalued.

A better insight into the real consequences for the economy as a whole of certain investments will therefore be gained if, instead of market prices, accounting prices are applied, implying, *inter alia,* that labor costs are assumed to be considerably lower than market wages indicate. This may lead to the execution of projects not attractive to the private investor, but attractive according to accounting prices.

It may seem unnatural to "calculate oneself rich" in this way. If in reality it is so "advantageous" to employ labor, where do these advantages show up and how, if only as an illustration of our recommendation, can the government realize them? The answer is that in a country with widespread unemployment a worker, when employed in a new investment project, becomes so much better off that he could, in principle, be taxed without a deterioration in his situation. More exactly still, not so much the worker, but his family (in the broader sense) which was feeding him, will experience this improvement. The government, of course, does not tax them since this would mean a discrimination against those previously unemployed as compared with those by coincidence not unemployed before. This in a way is equivalent, from the economic point of view, to a subsidy being paid to the worker; as, in fact, for the reason of the "fundamental disequilibrium," one is being paid by every employer to every worker. It is, therefore, not easy for the government to realize the advantages. Thus our conclusion is twofold. First, one of the beneficiaries is the previously unemployed worker and his family; since development policy is meant to be a contribution to the well-being of this group in particular this is not completely foolish. Secondly, however, the government as a rule foregoes certain theoretical tax receipts which it could otherwise have spent for further development. Put otherwise, the execution of the projects does absorb actual tax revenue. This sets a limit to either development at large or to the execution of "accounting price projects." An attempt to estimate the consequences and to take account of them in the national product test will be found in Annex v 3.

THE NATIONAL PRODUCT
(OR CONSUMPTION) TEST

Contents:

1. Nature of Problem; General Remarks
2. Principles to be Used in the Solution
3. Evaluating the Consequences of a Program
4. Choice and Use of Accounting Prices
5. An Illustration of the Estimation of Secondary Effects

1 *Nature of Problem; General Remarks*

The techniques recommended and, to an increasing degree, applied in the appraisal of investment projects are of a fairly complicated nature which justifies their being handled by specialists and
their treatment, for the purpose of this report, in a separate annex.

Even then there is a wide range of methods among which to
choose, according to the availability of data and experts to handle
them, and to the nature of the questions to be answered. It is not
the intention of this annex to give anything like a full treatment of
all these methods, but rather to stress certain of their aspects that
are accessible to still fairly simple calculations. Before trying to
give a systematic treatment we want to make it clear that in principle the problem at stake is rather complicated and that therefore
for practical purposes also, it "pays" to go into these questions.

We will not go into the preliminary question, already discussed in
the main text, whether the contribution to national income or the
contribution to some more general concept of welfare should be the
ultimate aim of the program. It will be assumed that national income (alternatively, national consumption) is the criterion. It
would not be difficult to generalize the method somewhat and to

take account of, e.g., the distribution of income or consumption over regions or over some classes of the population. Such generalization does require agreement, however, as to the quantitative importance of any shifts desired, which is clearly a political choice.

The complexity of the problem arises first of all from the fact that the effects of one project of the program are not independent of those of other projects, and that therefore it is the program rather than the individual project that should be considered. This is perhaps best illustrated by the quantity of scarce factors left for the rest of the economy: this depends on the whole program rather than on one project. Thus the choice is rather between alternative programs than between alternative projects. Often the simplification of considering the projects as mutually independent will be justified. This simplification is justified if each program is small enough not to influence the rest of the economy; but the programs to be considered are not always that small.

A second reason for complexity is found in the length of the period over which the consequences of a project have to be considered. It is hardly realistic to assume that the general economic situation will be constant during that period and it is essential that it should not be. It is again by some further simplification that the additions to national income can be considered to be independent of its size.

Both points so far discussed are illustrative of an important feature of the problem, namely, that it is a combination of the traditional type of appraisal, valid for small programs only, and of development planning. This is why there are as many possible methods of appraisal as there are methods of development planning itself. We shall not go into the more intricate problems of such planning, which are largely of a mathematical nature, and we shall make use of some of the simpler approaches only.

The third reason for the complexity of our problem is to be found in the factors that necessitate the use of accounting prices, mainly the existence of structural unemployment and of balance of payments difficulties. These factors are so real as to justify some extra trouble and it also seems feasible to apply accounting prices even if only a rough analysis is possible.

We will first try to formulate the problem in its most general way in order to show what the principles of the method should be; after that has been done, a few simplifications will be discussed that may make the method amenable to practical application.

2 *Principles to be Used in the Solution*

As already explained in the main text, the solution of the problem of appraising a project or a program of projects has to take into account first of all an estimation of its *consequences*. Essentially, this requires the comparison of two developments of the economy, development with and without (in the absence of) the program. If an exact model for the development of the economy concerned were available, two successive solutions of the system of equations of such a model should be determined. In the second solution all data referring to the program would be used; if the system of equations is exact, it would automatically yield the complete consequences—direct, indirect and secondary—and there is no reason to make a distinction between these types of consequences.

An exact system of equations does not exist, however; and if it existed it would be very complicated. It would be dynamic and micro-economic. For practical purposes, it will be necessary to simplify without, however, affecting essential features. Two problems then seem outstanding: what degree of *aggregation* can we apply and what simplified picture of *development* can we use? As to aggregation it seems natural to make a distinction at least between the program sectors and the rest of the economy. If the program consists of an electricity plant, the only corresponding sector is the one of building the plant and of producing electricity; if the program consists of a land reclamation project the reclamation process plus the production of wheat on the land may be the sector. Still another example might be the erection of a certain number of textile plants. There would be $n+1$ sectors (including the "rest" sector) if the program exists of "n" projects of "n" different types. If, among the "n" projects "m" would belong to the same type of activity, the number of sectors should be $n-m+2$.

Development in each of the sectors related to the program should be described in some detail by the equations, in fact in as much detail as is thought necessary for a true picture. Development in the "rest" sector may, however, appropriately be described in a simplified way. Here the assumption of a constant capital coefficient of the average size may be appropriate. The development of income in this sector would then be equal to the development of capital, divided by the capital coefficient. The development of capital would be a consequence of the process of saving. Savings might be assumed to be a given percentage of the "rest" sector income plus a varying ratio of income in each of the project sectors, depending on the nature of the projects. A possible influence of taxes on savings could also be easily brought into the picture. In the subsequent sections of this annex an example of the calculations will be given.

One particular consequence of the subdivision chosen is that possible future projects not explicitly specified at the moment of programming may be, in principle, part of the rest sector.

The next step consists of the *appraisal* of the consequences. This means the application to all physical elements of net income (i.e., output of products and input of factors) of accounting prices representing the "true value" of these products and factors. This step, therefore, raises the question of how to calculate accounting prices. In principle this calculation requires a "shadow development program," differing from the "real" program in that equilibria would be obtained by flexible pricing instead of, as may be the case in reality, by quantitative restrictions and rigid pricing. Thus, while in the real program balance of payments equilibrium may have been projected with the aid of quantitative restrictions on imports and without a change in exchange rates, in the shadow program it will have to be obtained by changes in exchange rates without quantitative restrictions. The same may be true with regard to savings [1] and the interest rates, with regard to scarce labor and the wage rate for such labor, etc. It may happen that for some reason no equilibrium can be obtained by flexible pricing alone (cf. Annex v 2); this may apply to the market for unskilled labor, usually in abundant supply. Capital may not be sufficient to employ all unskilled labor, even at zero price. The accounting price of such markets should be taken as equal to zero or only so much more as to account for the "displacement cost" (including psychological displacement); in all the other markets the flexible equilibrium price is taken to represent the accounting price.

From this definition it will be clear that accounting prices, at least in principle, can be estimated for complete programs only, not for separate projects, as has already been said.

The appraisal of the investment programs will then become possible by a calculation, year by year, of the accounting value of the additions to net income due to each of a set of alternative programs. Finally, the appraisal of the investment program must be summarized in the influence exerted on the *discounted "present" value of all future income* (or, alternatively, consumption). The discount rate to be applied is of considerable influence on the result and presents another example of the importance of the choice of accounting prices. Instead of income, consumption could have been taken. As a rule proportionality of consumption and income will be assumed—if only as an approximation—and then there is no need for this amendment. But the method presented may just as well be applied to consumption as to income.

Among all possible programs the one making the maximum con-

---

[1] There may be a complication here. There will be a difference between the capital needed on the basis of market prices of factors and products and that needed on the basis of accounting prices. For a calculation of the accounting price of capital, one should use the demand for capital based on the market prices of the other factors and of the products, since this is the demand actually to be exerted.

tribution to national income will finally have to be chosen; or, if consumption rather than income is taken as the criterion, the one with the maximum contribution to present and future consumption. Because of the tremendous work involved in evaluating the consequences of a program, it is of the utmost importance to have some guidance in the selection of programs before the appraisal on the basis of the national income (or consumption) test is undertaken. Such guidance should have the function of selecting projects likely to be optimal. It may refer to the type of product and its quantity as well as to technology to be applied. Some tentative rules were given in the main text (cf. Section IV 2). General programming will be one of the sources, since it may give some clues as to the market development to be expected as well as to the capital available per additional worker to be employed. It should be observed that, especially in this field, scientific development is fast and that new methods are being continually launched. Some of them are of a very complicated mathematical nature and require a large quantity of data; others are less exact and easier to handle. Again, what should be recommended will have to depend on the details of the situation in a given country.

3 *Evaluating the Consequences of a Program*

Having indicated the principles of a solution, we will now describe a simplified procedure that nevertheless seems to yield an essentially sound approximation in a number of cases.

For each project of a program, the succession of inputs and outputs for all future years will be considered given. This by itself, however, requires a program of analysis. It is not sufficient to know the input during the investment period, or the output and input during the operation period of the project proper. Indirect consequences will have to be collected, such as changes in the industries producing the raw materials needed for the project and changes in the industries using products of the project. Examples are given in the main text (cf. Section IV 3). It does not matter whether these changes are accompanied by flexible or by rigid prices in the markets concerned, but realistic assumptions have to be made. Another indirect consequence may be found in competing industries. All the changes so far considered may be summarized as primary or autonomous changes in the aggregated sector of the project considered. They have to be estimated for each project sector and the additions to national income so found will add up to the autonomous change in national income. The accounting prices to be used will be discussed separately. (Cf. Section 4 of this annex.)

The secondary or induced consequences have now to be evaluated. By this term is meant the consequences in the rest sector. As already observed, this evaluation may be made in a more or in a less sophisticated manner. Only a simple approach will be discussed here. More sophisticated methods require well-defined systems of equations and their solution. If we assume that net income in the rest sector is determined by the nation's capital (except the capital invested in the project sectors), an evaluation of this capital and the resulting income may be made. As already stated, the additions to this capital may be made by all sectors and this is the simplest way of interconnecting the sectors. The savings available in each sector will depend on the income and the type of income to be generated as well as on the capital requirements of the sectors themselves and the foreign assistance receivable. A first refinement may be made by the assumption that export values will depend on the quantities to be supplied and the corresponding price level of exports.

4 *Choice and Use of Accounting Prices*

As already stated (Section 2 of this annex), accounting prices have to be determined, in principle, by a cumbersome process of trial and error including "shadow programming." There seem to be approximations of a much simpler nature which are still relevant. Some of them will be discussed here. The simplest example is the one of the accounting price of unskilled labor. It will be possible to take this price as equal to zero in a good number of cases. Another not too difficult example is the accounting price for capital. An important indication of the influence of the price of capital may be obtained if an interest rate of some 10% is used alternatively to the rate at which, say, the International Bank for Reconstruction and Development makes loans.

A third example of an accounting price that may sometimes be estimated on *a priori* grounds would seem to be the rate of exchange, if there is a disequilibrium in the balance of payments. Sometimes estimates can be made, on the basis of an over-all model of the economy, not even showing separate sectors for each of the projects, of what exchange rate would seem to be an equilibrium rate.

A fourth example consists of the prices to be applied for individual commodities, if these commodities appear to be protected by import duties or quantitative restrictions. World market prices plus an average import duty for all commodities imported into the country will be a better approximation than the actual national price.

It may be repeated that even if it is not possible to make any sensible estimate of an accounting price, it may be useful to make a set of alternative calculations using plain guesses for the accounting prices. Such a set of calculations may show the influence exerted by changes in prices (cf. main text, Section IV 7).

The application of accounting prices without a complete "shadow program" should, of course, be a careful one and should at least be based on common sense consideration of the markets considered. Prices of scarce factors should not be taken to be equal to zero; sometimes a distinction between types of labor will be useful. Prices of products of which the supply is assumed to increase considerably as a consequence of the program under discussion should not be left unchanged. Sometimes demand studies may be available, giving some indication of the change in price to be expected from a given increase in supply.

5 *An Illustration of the Estimation of Secondary Effects*

As already observed, the complete calculation of all effects of a program requires the application of methods usually too difficult to be handled by the general economist and only worth while if rather extensive material is available. Often more or less approximate methods will have to be used. One possible method may be illustrated by the following scheme in which a number of elements have been inserted that were discussed in the previous sectors and the main text.

Example of a Scheme for the Estimation of the Effects on Future National Income (and Consumption) Exerted by a Program of Investment Projects

  A. Figures at market prices.
  B. Figures at accounting prices.
  C. Figures at accounting prices, discounted.

Line	Years	1	2	3	4	5	etc.	Total
		A B	A B C	A B C	A B C	A B C		C
	Sector 1, Direct							
101	Gross product							
102	Imports							
103	Depreciation							
104	Net product							
	(= 101 — 102 — 103)							
105	Scarce factors used							
	Indirect							
106	Gross product							

Line	Years	1	2	3	4	5	etc. Total
		A B	A B C	A B C	A B C	A B C	C
107	Imports						
108	Depreciation						
109	Net product ($=106 - 107 - 108$)						
110	Scarce factors used						
111	Primary $=$ dir. $+$ ———— indirect						
112	Net product ($=104 + 109$)						
113	Low incomes						
114	High incomes						
115	Gross savings						
116	Capital requirements						
117	Net savings ($=115 - 116$)						
	Sector 2,3 etc.						
201	etc. (Same subdivision)						
	Rest of Economy						
901	Savings previous year						
902	Influence of subsidies on government investments						
903	Net savings from other sectors ($117 + 217 + \ldots$)						
904	Total ($=901 - 902 + 903$)						
905	Capital, beginning						
906	Income (uncorrected)						
907	Correction for scarce factors ($=105 + 110 + 205 + \ldots$)						
908	Income rest of economy						
909	*Income, all sectors* ($=112 + 212 + \ldots + 908$)						
910	*Consumption, all sectors*						

The following explanations may be added.

It should be kept in mind that the scheme is one out of a large number of possibilities, none completely satisfactory.

The *number of years* depends on the rate of discount and can be less with higher discount rates than with lower rates. Sometimes the total over all years can be approximated by mathematical formulae, as, e.g., those for geometrical series.

Sectors are supposed to refer to projects.

Direct figures refer to production by project itself (cf. usual distinction in Kahn-Keynesian multiplier terminology).

Gross product (101) will be different for investment period and for operation period. Here it is defined as value added in process taking place each year.

Net product (104) is here defined as customary in national accounting, without deducting value of scarce national factors (skilled labor, technicians). Since these are, however, withdrawn from rest sector, a correction is made in items 105, 110, 205, etc., 908.

Scarce factors (105): see net product.

Indirect figures defined as in main text. Indirect figures may be superfluous if it is attempted to imply indirect consequences in the values given to accounting prices for the products and raw materials of the project.

"High" and "low" incomes (items 113 and 114) are supposed to be a breakdown of primary net product (112); the breakdown may be used to estimate the influence of the nature of the project on the nation's rate of savings.

Gross savings (115) are the savings originating from 114.

Capital requirements are the capital needed in the sector, after correction for possible capital imports.

Net savings (117) are available for the rest of the economy.

Sectors 2,3, etc. represent other projects of the program. If only one project is studied and if it is assumed that accounting prices can be applied independently of other projects, these sectors do not appear in the scheme. The rest of the economy sector should always be included, however, since it is the bearer, in this scheme, of all secondary consequences.

Rest of economy represents a simplified picture of all other sectors, using macro-economic concepts and relations.

Savings previous year are savings in rest sector, to be estimated on the basis of the income to the rest of the economy (908), with the help of a general savings rate (meant to include government savings).

Subsidies, possibly paid by government (cf. main text, Section v 4) to further labor-intensive activities, may reduce government investment itself (by the full amount of subsidies or by part only).

Net savings from other sectors represent the influence exerted by type of project on general savings.

Total savings (previous year) accruing to rest sector (904) is the addition to capital of rest sector at beginning of year of reporting; it is supposed to be the chief determinant of income of the rest sector (in accordance with capital coefficient theory).

Income (uncorrected) (906) to be derived from capital, by division through capital coefficient (cf. Annex v 1).

Correction for scarce factors. The uncorrected income estimate may need correction for the fact that scarce factors will be withdrawn from the rest sector. One way of correcting this may be the deduction of the value of scarce factors from the uncorrected estimate (906). This implies a certain hypothesis as to the nature of the production function, however. Other hypotheses may be better, e.g., the assumption that scarce factors are a bottleneck and hence also restrict the use that can be made of other factors.

Income, all sectors (909) represents a national income estimate. Its value in column total, C, is the criterion for the appraisal of a project or program according to national income test.

Consumption, all sectors (910) might be taken instead, since it does not imply double counting of investment.

ANNEX V 4   SOME FIGURES ON INVESTMENTS
IN TRANSPORTATION AS A PERCENTAGE
OF TOTAL INVESTMENTS

I. *Long-term movements in the United States*
   Percentage of national wealth invested in railways, shipping and canals:

1880	1890	1900	1912	1922	1939
28.5	26.6	27.0	25.1	22.2 [1]	22 to 23 [2]

   Source: S. Kuznets, *National Product Since 1869* (1880-1922)
             W. Leontief cf. *Studies in the Structure of the American Economy,* 1953 (1939). With correction for automobiles.

II. *Recent figures for two underdeveloped countries*
    India, 1951-56: 20 *Source:* First Five Year Plan, p. 36-39
    Mexico, 1939-1950: 27 *Source:* The Economic Development of Mexico, Baltimore, 1953, p. 189, 201.

[1] Figure given by Kuznets (*op. cit.*) excludes motor cars, but is supposed to be too high (cf. Leontief, *op. cit.*, p. 218).
[2] Inclusive of the estimated value of motor cars.

III. *Recent figures for some European countries*

Average percentage (for 4 to 5 post-war years) of gross investment devoted to railways (including tramways), shipping, air transportation, motor traffic and communications:

Belgium	24
Norway	30
United Kingdom	17
Netherlands	23
France	19

Source: Economic Survey of Europe Since the War, United Nations, corrected to make strictly comparable.

INDEX

Index

accounting prices, 34, 36, 38, 41–42, 53, 80–81, 82–83, 83n; application of, 86–87; and appraisal of investment projects, 39–41; calculation of, 82–83, 85–86; defined, 40; and fundamental disequilibria, 76–78

A.K.U. (Netherlands rayon corporation), 62

alternative programs, 11, 16, 80, 83

appraisal of investment projects. *See* national product (or consumption) test; private investment; public investment

balance of payments disequilibrium, 5, 39–40, 76, 86

Belgium, investment in transportation, 91

bottlenecks, economic, 8, 26–27

capital: definition of, 70–71; per person employed, 24, 71–72, *Table,* 73; scarcity of, 49, 77

capital coefficients, 13–16, 70–76, 82; of American industries, *Table,* 72; definition of concept, 70–71; for national economies, *Table,* 74; and savings rates, 15; and statistical

sources, 15–16; for underdeveloped countries, 13, 75–76

capital intensity, 13, 32, 34, 49, 50, 71, 72–73

capital-output ratio, 71, 73–75; *see also* capital coefficients

Central Institute for Industrialization, Netherlands, 57

Clark, Colin, 17n, 74n

competition, international, 18

complementarity, 31–32

consistency conditions in development, 9, 10

consumer goods, demand data on, 17

cost, comparative, principle of, 19

cost estimates: and private investment projects, 47–48; testing of, 21, 22–24

cottage industries, 37–38, 53

data and information, 5–6, 9–10; on alternative production methods, 24; demand data, sources of, 17; quality of, influence on programming, 27; as stimulant to private investment, 55–57; *see also* cost estimates; demand analysis; market analysis; statistics

95